· m i c r o w a v e ·
CHINESE
COOKING

・ *microwave* ・
CHINESE
COOKING

Traditional Recipes for the Modern Cook

◆ DEH-TA HSIUNG ◆

Macdonald Orbis

A *Macdonald Orbis* Book
© 1988
First published in Great Britain in 1988
by Macdonald & Co (Publishers) Ltd
London & Sydney

A member of Pergamon MCC Publishing Corporation plc

British Library Cataloguing in Publication Data
Hsuing, Deh-Ta
Microwave Chinese Cooking.
1. Cookery, Chinese 2. Microwave
cookery
I. Title
641.5′882′0951   TX724.5.C5

ISBN 0–356–14857–2

Typeset by Bookworm, Salford
Printed and bound in Great Britain by Purnell Book Production Limited

Illustrations by Ian Hand

Editor: Catherine Rubinstein
Art Editor: Clive Hayball
Designer: Christopher Branfield
Photographer: Nick Carmen
Stylist: Sue Russell-Fell
Home Economist: Sarah Bush
Indexer: Alexandra Corrin

Macdonald & Co (Publishers) Ltd
Greater London House
Hampstead Road
London NW1 7QX

ACKNOWLEDGEMENTS
I would like to thank Lewis Esson who first suggested to me that I should
write a microwave cookbook for Chinese food. I am greatly indebted to
Caroline Young for her enthusiastic help and advice. And I also wish to
thank the following companies for their kindness in providing equipment
used in testing the recipes for this book:
SAMSUNG Electronics (UK) Ltd
PANASONIC (UK) Ltd
ANCHOR HOCKING CORPORATION

CONTENTS

◆

FOREWORD

AT FIRST THOUGHT THE idea of writing a microwave Chinese cookbook might appear to be heresy. The Chinese have an age-old tradition of cooking their food in utensils, such as iron woks and clay casseroles, that have remained unchanged for centuries, and of relying mostly on natural resources – wood, charcoal, coke and gas – for fuel. Furthermore, most Chinese kitchens are equipped with simple stoves but no ovens, so most roasting and baking is done by professional cooks, as it requires the skill of a master craftsman to operate the kiln-like Chinese ovens.

In the microwave oven you have a highly sophisticated piece of equipment that cooks food by molecular agitation, is comparatively simple to operate, and apart from roasting and baking, can also be used for steaming, poaching and braising. In addition, it reduces conventional cooking time by as much as 40–60 per cent.

On looking closer, however, one soon realizes that microwaves and Chinese cooking have more in common than meets the eye; take, for instance, the microwave's ability to cook vegetables without destroying their natural colour, flavour or nutritional value, and all done in a matter of minutes – precisely the result achieved by the unique Chinese cooking methods of stir-frying and quick-braising, but more healthily, because much less fat is used. If you prefer traditional cooking methods, stir-fried dishes cooked in a wok can be reheated in a microwave without losing any flavour or texture. This is particularly useful if you want to serve three or four dishes simultaneously, all piping hot. Alternatively, food cooked in large quantities can be frozen, then thawed in a microwave oven in minutes when required.

Do not think that I am abandoning my ancient tradition entirely in favour of modern technology. No, far from exchanging my wok for a microwave oven, I merely wish to extend the range of dishes I can produce in a small kitchen or within a limited time. No one is suggesting that a microwave oven can replace the conventional oven or cooking stove in all its functions in a Western kitchen; similarly, do not expect to cook all Chinese food by microwave. I have created and tested the recipes in this book almost entirely by microwave cooking. But if you are experienced with the conventional methods of Chinese cooking, you will have no difficulty in adapting these recipes to your own methods.

All in all, I am convinced there is a great future for microwaves in Chinese cookery. I am tempted to rewrite Rudyard Kipling's often-quoted maxim thus: 'Oh, East is East, and West is West, but the twain *shall* meet . . . in a microwave oven!'

Deh-Ta Hsiung, London, 1987

INTRODUCTION

IF YOU ARE THE PROUD owner of a microwave oven, you are probably quite familiar with its workings and know what type of cookware should or should not be used. For this reason you will find no such information in this book. If in doubt, consult the manufacturer's instruction booklet supplied with your oven.

One of the difficulties in writing a microwave cookbook is that ovens vary in their power and settings. For instance, HIGH OR FULL power on one model may be 500 watts, while on another it could be 700 watts. Since the majority of microwave ovens on the market are between 600 and 650 watts, I have based all my recipes on this output:

HIGH/FULL/100% = 600–650 watts
MEDIUM/ROAST/70% = 420–455 watts
LOW/DEFROST/30% = 180–195 watts

If your oven has a lower power output, allow a longer cooking time for the recipes. (Consult the manufacturer's instruction booklet.)

THE MAIN CHARACTERISTICS OF CHINESE CUISINE

The most distinctive feature of Chinese cuisine is the harmonious blending of different colours, aromas, flavours, shapes and textures in one single dish. The principle of blending complementary or contrasting colours and flavours is a fundamental one and different ingredients must not be mixed indiscriminately; the matching process should follow a set pattern and be controlled, not casual.

The cutting of ingredients is another important element in Chinese cuisine: in order to achieve the proper effect, slices are matched with slices, shreds with shreds, cubes with cubes, chunks with chunks, and so on. This is not only for the sake of appearance, but also because ingredients of the same size and shape require about the same amount of cooking time.

The interrelation of colours, flavours and shapes in Chinese cuisine is reinforced by yet another feature: texture. A dish may have just one, or several contrasting textures, such as tenderness, crispiness, smoothness and softness. Sogginess, stringiness and hardness have no place in Chinese cooking. The desired texture or textures in any dish can only be achieved by the correct degree of heat and cooking time.

ACHIEVING HARMONY AND CONTRAST

A Chinese dish is usually made up of more than one ingredient because if there is no contrast it is hard to create harmony. Some cooks like to mix completely contrasting flavours and unrelated textures, other prefer the matching of similar tastes and colours. Some wish to preserve the flavour of each ingredient, while others believe in the infusion of flavours. The principles of harmony and contrast are quite straightforward. First you choose the 'main' ingredient, then decide what type or types of supplementary ingredients will go best with it, bearing in mind the differences of colour, flavour, texture and so on. For instance, if the main ingredient is chicken breast meat, which is white in colour and tender in texture, one could choose something pale and crisp, like celery, as a supplementary ingredient, or perhaps something more colourful, like crisp green or red peppers, or something soft like mushrooms.

CUTTING TECHNIQUES

The Chinese practice of cutting food into small, neat pieces before cooking stems partly from fuel conservation and partly from the fact that small pieces of food are easier to serve and eat with chopsticks; knives and carvers have not been used on Chinese tables since ancient times. Of course, small pieces of food only require a short cooking time, so they also retain their natural flavour and nutritional value.

The following are the standard sizes and shapes in Chinese cooking:

Slice Slices are thin, flat pieces. Cut the ingredient into sections, as required by the dimensions of the slices, then slice the sections to the desired thickness. Diagonal slicing is recommended in certain recipes to speed the cooking process. The size often determines the cooking time.

Strip, Shred Strips and shreds are similar in shape but different in size; strips are quite thick (perhaps 1 cm/½ in), while shreds are very thin, and very finely shredded ingredients are literally the size of matchsticks. First cut the ingredient into slices, then pile them on top of each other like a pack of playing cards, and cut them into strips or shreds, as required.

Chunk, Piece There are many kinds of chunks and pieces: diamonds, hexagons, rectangles or wedges. First cut the ingredient into broad strips or sections, and then into smaller pieces, as required.

Dice, Cube Dice and small cubes are pieces cut from strips.

Grain, Mince Grains are finely chopped ingredients cut from shreds. Mince is even finer and is cut by much chopping and pressing with the flat of the blade.

In addition to these techniques are **Flower-cutting** and **Scoring**, often used for thick ingredients, such as kidney, squid and fish, in order to allow more heat and sauce penetration. These techniques are described in the recipes where they apply.

CHOPPING A COOKED CHICKEN OR DUCK

1 Detach the two wings at the breast, then cut each wing into two pieces at the joint; discard the wing tips.

2 Detach the thighs by cutting through the skin around the joints with a sharp knife or the tip of a cleaver. Separate the legs (drumsticks) from the thighs through the joints, one at a time.

3 Lay the limbless bird on its side and separate the breasts from the backbone section by cutting down through the soft bone from the tail to the neck.

4 Carve away the meat and skin from the backbone and ribcage, cut into small bite-size pieces and arrange them in a straight row down the centre of an oval serving platter.

5 Lay the bird breast-side down and remove the wishbone and main breastbone by hand. Turn the meat over so the skin side is now facing upward; cut the two breasts in half lengthways, then chop each breast crossways into small, neat pieces. Transfer the breast meat pieces to the serving platter, one half at a time, and arrange them on top of the backbone meat.

6 Chop the legs and thighs crossways into small bite-size pieces and arrange them on each side of the breast halves. Arrange the two wings, one on each side, near the upper part of the breast meat, so that the original shape of the chicken or duck is now approximated.

MARINATING

The purpose of marinating is to enhance the flavours of poultry, meat and fish. White meats and fish are marinated in salt, egg white and cornflour, in order to preserve the natural delicate texture of the food when cooked in hot oil. Red meats are usually marinated in salt, sugar, soy sauce, rice wine and cornflour, and the longer you can leave the meat in the marinade, the better.

CHINESE COOKING METHODS

There are well over forty different cooking methods in Chinese cuisine, and they fall roughly into the following categories:

Water cooking Boiling, poaching and simmering
Oil cooking Deep-frying, shallow-frying, stir-frying and braising
Fire cooking Roasting, baking and barbecuing
Steam cooking Steaming

Apart from deep-frying, baking and barbecuing, all the other cooking methods can be carried out in a microwave oven.

EQUIPMENT

I find the most versatile piece of cookware for Chinese food is a *large, round casserole with a vented lid,* made from materials specially suited to microwave cooking. It can be used for everything from stock- and soup-making to stir-frying and braising; get two or three sizes.

The next most useful item is an *all-purpose cooker* or *multi-purpose cook set* which usually consists of a base dish, a ribbed rack and a cover. It is ideal for steaming or roasting, and the lid can also be used as a casserole.

In order to achieve the crisp, golden finish required in certain recipes, a *browning dish,* sometimes called a *browning skillet* or *browning griddle,* is essential. Although it is probably the most expensive single item apart from the oven itself, you will find it invaluable. Alternatively, of course, you can finish off the dish under the grill.

MENU
PLANNING

THERE ARE CERTAIN QUALITIES that distinguish Chinese cooking from
that of most other cultures. To start with, we make the distinction,
when preparing and serving a meal, between *fan* (grains and other
starch foods) and *cai* (meat and vegetable dishes). Grain, in the form of
rice or wheat-flour (bread, pancakes, noodles or dumplings), makes up
the *fan* part of the meal. Vegetables, meat, poultry and fish, which are
usually cut up and combined in individual dishes, constitute the *cai*
part. A balanced meal must have appropriate amounts of *fan* and *cai*.

A harmonious balance is, of course, also important in terms of
colours, aromas, flavours and textures, as well as shapes and forms –
and this applies as much to the various courses served during a meal as
to each single dish. People in the West are often puzzled by this aspect
of serving Chinese food, particularly because the order of courses
served at a Chinese meal bears no resemblance to the Western sequence
of soup-fish-poultry-meat-cheese-dessert.

The traditions of Chinese cuisine affect the whole pattern of life: the
Chinese way of eating creates a feeling of togetherness and harmony, as
we gather around a table and share all the dishes in communal style.
(The Chinese never serve an individual dish to each person). Indeed,
Chinese food is best eaten communally, for only then can you enjoy a
variety of dishes. The only exception is for a light snack, when
everybody will be given a dish of *chow mein* or a bowl of noodles in
soup.

When it comes to planning quantities allow one dish per person, but
two dishes should be enough for 3–4 people, three dishes for 4–6
people, four dishes for 6–8, and so on. An informal Chinese dinner
served at home is essentially a buffet-style affair, with more hot dishes
than cold served at the same time and shared by everyone. Only at
formal dinner parties or banquets are dishes served singly, or in groups
course by course. The order in which different courses or dishes are
served depends more on the methods of preparation and cooking than
on the food itself.

A typical dinner menu for 10–12 people would consist of 6–8 dishes
served in the following order:

◆

FIRST COURSE
2–3 cold starters or an assorted hors d'oeuvre dish

◆

SECOND COURSE
2–3 stir-fried or quick-braised dishes, which should always be 'dry'

rather than full of gravy. The exact number and variety of dishes are flexible; it all depends on the scale of the occasion, or what was served before and what is to follow.

◆

MAIN COURSE

1, 2, or 3 'big' dishes; these can be steamed, long-braised (red-cooked) or roasted but usually consist of a whole chicken, duck, fish and joint of meat. Rice and/or noodles are served with the main course.

◆

DESSERT

Only served at formal banquets in China; soup is often served for less grand occasions. As a compromise, fresh fruit and China tea can always be served at the end of a big Chinese meal instead of pudding.

Specific menu suggestions for various occasions are on p. 115. A Chinese meal is served absolutely ready to eat – there is no last-minute carving, or dishing out of separate items such as vegetables, gravy or sauce. Everyone can start eating at the same time.

WHAT TO DRINK WITH CHINESE FOOD

Do not serve tea or water with Chinese food. In China soup is usually served throughout an everyday meal in order to help wash down the bulky and savoury food. When it comes to formal dinners or entertaining, wine and spirits are essential parts of the fare.

As each course of a Chinese meal usually consists of a number of different dishes, it is almost impossible to match a particular wine with a particular dish. I just do not understand why some people regard only white wine as suitable with Chinese food. Obviously a white is a perfect partner for cold starters and some lightly-seasoned fried dishes, but for the more strongly flavoured main courses you really need a wine that has plenty of body as well as bite. A good white wine of that calibre would cost you a small fortune, but there is a wide choice of smooth and fruity reds that are good value for money. By all means start your meal with white wine, then go on to red if there are enough people eating to warrant opening more than one bottle. For smaller numbers I would recommend a light, fruity red, such as a good Beaujolais, Mâcon or Côtes-du-Rhône; a red from the Loire, such as Chinon or Bourgueil; Californian Cabernet Sauvignon or Pinot Noir; Italian Valpolicella or Bardolino; or Spanish Rioja. As for good quality whites, the best bet is to stick to the grape variety: Riesling, Sauvignon and Chardonnay.

All the recipes in this book serve 4, provided they are served with a second dish at the same time.

SOUPS

IN CHINA SOUP IS NOT *regarded as a separate course, except at banquets and other formal occasions. At an everyday meal in Chinese homes, a simple soup is served with all the other dishes and usually consists of a clear broth with a few thinly sliced or shredded vegetables and/or meat.*

A good stock is essential to a successful soup, but as it requires long, slow simmering to bring out the flavour, it is best made in the conventional way on top of the stove. However, small quantities of chicken and pork sparerib stock can be successfully made in a microwave.

If stock is unavailable, a Chinese cook can make a soup fit for the gods merely be adding any available ingredients to boiling water and pouring the result over seasonings in a serving bowl. Should you use a chicken or beef stock cube as a substitute, remember to reduce the amount of seasoning in recipes, as cubes usually contain a lot of salt.

All the soup recipes in this section can also be cooked in a saucepan or wok on the top of a conventional stove, but the cooking time will have to be doubled or even trebled in certain cases.

BASIC STOCK FOR CLEAR SOUP

Besides being the basis for soup-making, a good stock is also used instead of water whenever a recipe requires liquid. Any leftover stock should be refrigerated, and will keep for around 4–5 days; alternatively, it can be frozen in small containers and thawed out in the required amount.

◆

675 g/1½ lb chicken pieces
450 g/1 lb pork spareribs or bones
6 cm/3 in piece ginger root, unpeeled and cut into chunks
2–3 spring onions, trimmed
2.75 litres/5 pt water
45–60 ml/3–4 tbsp Shao Hsing rice wine or dry sherry (optional)

◆

1 Trim off excess fat from the chicken and pork. Place the meat in a large casserole and add the ginger root, spring onions and water. Bring to the boil on HIGH and boil for 6–10 minutes. Skim off any scum.
2 Cover with a vented lid and cook on MEDIUM for 40–60 minutes.
3 Strain the stock, discarding the chicken, pork, ginger and spring onions; add the wine, return it to the microwave and bring to the boil again on HIGH. Cook for 40–50 seconds. Use as stock or add seasonings, such as salt and pepper, and serve as a clear soup. Allow about 175 ml/6 fl oz per person.

CHINESE LEAVES AND MUSHROOM SOUP

After the meat and skin are removed from Roast Duck Peking-Style (see p.85), its carcass is made into a soup with Chinese leaves and mushrooms to be served at the end of the meal. This is really only practical for restaurants, since there will always be a spare duck carcass to make the soup with, long before you have finished eating; at home you would have to wait for a good hour before the soup would be ready. Therefore, I suggest that you keep the carcass to make the soup for another day.

◆

4–6 dried Chinese mushrooms
1 duck carcass (plus giblets if available)
2 small pieces ginger root
450 g/1 lb Chinese leaves
salt and pepper
fresh coriander to garnish

◆

1 Put the mushrooms to soak in warm water for 20–25 minutes.
2 Break up the carcass, place it with the giblets and ginger in a large casserole, then cover with water (about 2 l/3½ pt). Bring to the boil on HIGH. Skim the surface, cover with a vented lid and cook on MEDIUM for 30–45 minutes.
3 Squeeze the mushrooms dry, discard the hard stalks and cut the mushrooms into thin slices.
4 Wash the Chinese leaves and cut into 2.5 cm/1 in slices; add to the soup with the sliced mushrooms and cook on HIGH for 2–3 minutes. Adjust the seasoning. Garnish with fresh coriander and serve hot.

Top: Bean curd and Spinach Soup (page 19); *centre:* Seafood and Asparagus Soup (page 19); *bottom:* Three-flavour Soup (page 20)

PRAWN AND BEAN CURD SOUP

Colour and nutrition are deliciously combined in this soup. For best results, use raw prawns; if using ready-cooked prawns, add them to the stock at the last minute, as they only need to be warmed through.

◆

50 g/2 oz peeled prawns
½ egg white, lightly beaten
1 cake bean curd
600 ml/1 pt stock
50 g/2 oz peas
5 ml/1 tsp Shao Hsing rice wine or dry sherry
15 ml/1 tbsp light soy sauce
5 ml/1 tsp each of finely chopped spring onions and ginger root
5 ml/1 tsp sesame seed oil
salt and pepper

◆

1 Mix the prawns with the egg white. Cut the bean curd into small cubes roughly the same size as the peas.

2 Place the stock in a casserole and bring to the boil on HIGH (2–6 minutes). Add the raw prawns and bean curd and cook for 30 seconds. Add the peas, wine and soy sauce, and cook for another 40–50 seconds.

3 Stir in the spring onions, ginger root, sesame seed oil and seasonings. Serve hot.

EGG-DROP SOUP

This must be about the simplest method of making a soup, and most economical as well, since a single egg can be made to serve up to six people! However, we will not be so frugal just this once, but use two eggs to make four helpings.

◆

600 ml/1 pt stock
2 eggs
salt
15 ml/1 tbsp finely chopped spring onions

◆

1 Place the stock in a serving bowl and bring to a rolling boil on HIGH. This will take about 2–6 minutes, depending on the initial temperature of the stock.

2 Beat the eggs with a pinch of salt, then pour very, very slowly into the boiling stock, stirring constantly. Add salt to taste and garnish with spring onions. Serve hot.

FISH SLICES AND LETTUCE SOUP

A generous seasoning of white pepper makes this warming soup from northern China an ideal dish for cold winter nights. The lettuce can be substituted with Chinese leaves, watercress or spinach.

◆

225 g/8 oz white fish fillet, such as plaice or lemon sole
15 ml/1 tbsp cornflour
1 egg white, lightly beaten
1 lettuce heart
about 600 ml/1 pt stock or water
5 ml/1 tsp finely chopped ginger root (optional)
15 ml/1 tbsp vinegar
salt
white pepper
finely chopped spring onions to garnish

◆

1 Cut the fish into slices about the size of a matchbox. Dust with cornflour, then coat with egg white.

2 Wash the lettuce and cut the leaves into thin shreds.

3 Place the stock or water in a casserole and bring to the boil on HIGH (2–6 minutes). Add the fish slices, ginger and vinegar. Cook on MEDIUM for 2 minutes, or until the soup starts to boil again, then add the lettuce, and cook for about 1 minute longer. Season with salt and lots of pepper. Garnish with spring onions and serve hot.

CHICKEN AND BEANSPROUT SOUP

There are clear and thick versions of this soup. The thick soup is really a Western invention in which it is not necessary to use stock at all; egg whites and cornflour are simply added to plain water.

◆

115–150 g/4–5 oz chicken breast meat, skinned and boned
115 g/4 oz fresh beansprouts
600 ml/1 pt stock or water
2–3 egg whites (optional)
15 ml/1 tbsp cornflour mixed with 15 ml/1 tbsp cold water (optional)
salt
a few drops of sesame seed oil
finely chopped spring onions to garnish

◆

1 Thinly shred the chicken meat.

2 Wash the beansprouts in cold water, discard the husks and any little bits that float to the surface (it is not necessary to top and tail each sprout).

3 Place the stock or water in a casserole and bring to the boil on HIGH (2–6 minutes). While waiting, comb the egg whites with your fingers to loosen them, and mix the cornflour and water to a smooth paste.

4 Add the chicken to the boiling liquid, stir and cook for 2 more minutes to bring back to boil. Add the beansprouts and pour in the egg whites very slowly, stirring constantly. Add salt to taste and thicken the soup with the cornflour paste, if using. Cook on MEDIUM for 40–50 seconds.

5 Sprinkle with sesame seed oil, garnish with spring onions and serve hot.

Top: Chinese Cabbage and Mushroom Soup (page 14); *centre:* Sweetcorn and Crabmeat
Soup (page 21); *bottom:* Sliced Lamb and Cucumber Soup (page 20)

BEAN CURD AND SPINACH SOUP

In China this highly nutritious and popular soup is given the rather poetic name of 'Emerald and White Jade Soup'. When spinach is not in season, substitute any other tender green vegetable, such as cabbage, lettuce or watercress.

◆

1 cake bean curd
115 g/4 oz spinach leaves (prepared weight)
600 ml/1 pt stock
15 ml/1 tbsp light soy sauce
salt

◆

1 Cut the bean curd into 12 small slices about 5 mm/¼ in thick.
2 Wash the spinach thoroughly, separating the leaves and discarding the tough stems.
3 Bring the stock to a rolling boil on HIGH (2–6 minutes, depending on the temperature of the stock). Add the bean curd and spinach. Cook on MEDIUM for about 1 minute. (Lettuce and watercress only require 30–40 seconds' cooking.) Skim the surface so that it is clear, add the seasonings and stir well. Serve hot.

SEAFOOD AND ASPARAGUS SOUP

The original recipe for this soup from southern China calls for abalone. I think you will agree that abalone is an acquired taste, besides being extremely expensive, so I have substituted scallops. If asparagus is out of season mange-tout, lettuce hearts or watercress may be used instead.

◆

115 g/4 oz peeled prawns, preferably uncooked
115 g/4 oz scallops
115 g/4 oz asparagus
900 ml/1½ pt stock
salt
finely chopped spring onions to garnish

◆

1 If the prawns are large, cut into 2 or 3 pieces. Cut each scallop into quarters.
2 Discard the tough ends of the asparagus, then cut the tender spears into short lengths diagonally.
3 Place the stock in a casserole and bring to the boil on HIGH (3–6 minutes). Add the asparagus and cook on MEDIUM for 2 minutes (mange-tout requires only 1 minute, while lettuce hearts and watercress need less than 1 minute).
4 Add the prawns and scallops, cook for another minute at the very most. Add salt and serve hot, garnished with finely chopped spring onions.

THREE-FLAVOUR SOUP

Any kind of shellfish, such as scallops, crab, oysters, clams or lobster, can be substituted for the prawns in this recipe. Similarly, pork fillet can be used instead of chicken or ham.

◆

115 g/4 oz chicken breast meat, skinned and boned
½ egg white, lightly beaten
5 ml/1 tsp cornflour mixed with a little cold water
115 g/4 oz peeled prawns
115 g/4 oz cooked ham
600 ml/1 pt stock
5 ml/1 tsp Shao Hsing rice wine or dry sherry
salt and pepper
5 ml/1 tsp finely chopped spring onions

◆

1 Thinly slice the chicken into small pieces, then mix with the egg white and cornflour.
2 If the prawns are large, cut each into 2 or 3 pieces, and finely chop the ham.
3 Place the stock in a casserole and bring to the boil on HIGH (2–6 minutes). Add the chicken, prawns and ham, and cook for 30–40 seconds.
4 Adjust the seasoning and garnish with the spring onions. Serve hot.

SLICED LAMB AND CUCUMBER SOUP

From Peking comes this simple variation of the popular hot and sour soup.

◆

225 g/8 oz leg of lamb fillet
15 ml/1 tbsp Shao Hsing rice wine or dry sherry
15 ml/1 tbsp light soy sauce
5 ml/1 tsp sesame seed oil (optional)
½ cucumber
600 ml/1 pt stock
15 ml/1 tbsp vinegar
salt and pepper

◆

1 Trim off any excess fat from the lamb. Cut the meat into very thin slices about the size of a large postage stamp. Marinate with the wine, soy sauce and sesame seed oil, if using, for about 20–25 minutes.
2 Split the cucumber in half lengthways, then cut it across into thin slices. Do not peel.
3 Bring the stock to a rolling boil on HIGH (2–6 minutes). Add the lamb and stir to separate the slices. Cook on HIGH for 30 seconds. As soon as the soup starts to boil again, add the vinegar and cucumber, then cook on MEDIUM for 40–50 seconds.
4 Pour the soup over the seasonings in a heated tureen, stir well and serve hot.

BEEF AND TOMATO SOUP

This is a Cantonese soup which is very easy to make and extremely nourishing.

◆

115 g/4 oz beef steak
10 ml/2 tsp light soy sauce
15 ml/1 tbsp Shao Hsing rice or dry sherry
5 ml/1 tsp sugar
15 ml/1 tbsp cornflour mixed with 15 ml/1 tbsp cold water
225 g/8 oz firm tomatoes
600 ml/1 pt stock or water
a few drops of sesame seed oil
salt and pepper
finely chopped spring onions to garnish

◆

1 Thinly slice the beef.
2 Mix together the soy sauce, wine, sugar and cornflour paste and marinate the beef in the mixture for 10–15 minutes, longer if possible.
3 Skin the tomatoes, if you wish, then cut into small pieces.
4 Place the stock or water in a casserole and bring to the boil on HIGH (2–6 minutes). Add the beef and tomatoes, cook for 30–40 seconds, then add the oil, salt and pepper.
5 Place the garnish in a tureen, pour over the hot soup and serve.

SWEETCORN AND CRABMEAT SOUP

You have undoubtedly seen this soup on the menu in many Cantonese Chinese restaurants, but did you know that it originated in the West? It has recently been introduced to China and is well received there. Coarsley minced chicken breast can be used instead of crabmeat, if you prefer.

◆

115 g/4 oz crabmeat, thawed if frozen
5 ml/1 tsp finely chopped ginger root
2 egg whites
15 ml/1 tbsp cornflour
30–45 ml/2–3 tbsp milk
900 ml/1½ pt stock
225 g/8 oz can creamed sweetcorn
salt and pepper
finely chopped spring onions to garnish

◆

1 Flake the crabmeat, then mix it with the ginger.
2 Beat the egg whites in a bowl until frothy, add the milk and cornflour and beat again until smooth. Stir in the crabmeat.
3 Bring the stock to the boil on HIGH (3–6 minutes), add the sweetcorn and cook for 1 more minute, or until it starts to boil again.
4 Gently stir in the egg mixture and mix well to combine. Cook on MEDIUM for 1–1½ minutes, or until the soup thickens. Adjust the seasoning. Garnish with the spring onions and serve hot.

STARTERS

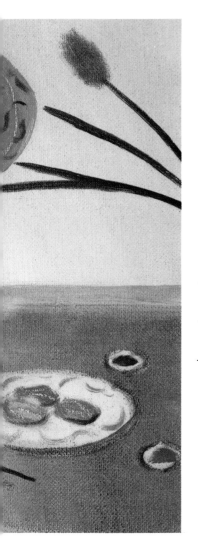

CHINA HAS AN IMMENSE VARIETY *of dishes that are served at the beginning of a meal. Like hors d'oeuvres or antipasti, these dishes are generally small and simple, but they can be quite elaborate and even spectacular for a special occasion or a formal dinner.*

One of the advantages of these dishes is that, since most of them are served cold, they can be prepared and cooked well in advance – hours or even days beforehand. Another advantage is that when cooked in fairly large quantities, any leftovers can be served on another occasion, either on their own, or in combination with other dishes. Of course, most of these dishes are ideal for buffet-style meals or party food.

For reasons of hygiene the Chinese seldom eat raw vegetables, partly because manure is used extensively as fertilizer. Most Chinese 'salad' dishes are pre-cooked (usually by blanching or par-boiling), then served cold with dressing. Since most vegetables contain a large amount of water, particularly when fresh, they can be cooked in the microwave with no extra liquid in a matter of seconds, thus retaining much of their nutritional value.

Obviously, vegetables grown in the West and by modern methods are quite safe to be eaten raw.

SHANGHAI SOYA DUCK

This was one of my favourites as a cold starter in China, but unfortunately I have never seen it on any restaurant's menu in the West.

◆

2 kg/4½–4¾ lb duckling
10 ml/2 tsp salt
1.25 ml/¼ tsp red powder (optional)
5–6 star anise or 5 ml/1 tsp aniseed
2–3 sticks cinnamon
3–4 spring onions
3–4 pieces ginger root
115 g/4 oz rock candy or crystal sugar
75 ml/5 tbsp Shao Hsing rice wine or brandy
30 ml/2 tbsp light soy sauce
75 ml/5 tbsp dark soy sauce
15 ml/1 tbsp sesame seed oil

◆

1 Clean the duck well and calculate the cooking time based on 7–10 minutes to 450 g/1 lb.
2 Place the duck in a large casserole, cover with boiling water and cook on HIGH for 2 minutes.
3 Drain the duck, discarding the liquid; rinse the bird under cold water and pat dry. Rub the cavity of the duck with the salt.
4 Place the red powder, star anise and cinnamon in a muslin bag and drop it into 600 ml/1 pt fresh boiling water in the casserole; bring to the boil and cook on HIGH for 3–5 minutes; by then the water should have turned red.
5 Remove the bag and put the duck in the water, breast side down. Add the spring onions, ginger root, sugar, wine and soy sauce. Cover with a vented lid and cook on HIGH for half the cooking time.
6 Turn the duck over, replace the lid and complete the cooking.
7 Remove the duck from the casserole, rub it all over with sesame seed oil and cover lightly with foil. Leave to stand.
8 Boil the cooking liquid, uncovered, until it has reduced by one-third – about 5 minutes. Baste the duck with the sauce several times.
9 Chop the duck into small, bite-size pieces (see p.8) and serve either on its own, or as one of several hors d'oeuvres.

BEANSPROUT SALAD

In most run-of-the-mill Chinese restaurants, virtually every dish on the menu will contain the ubiquitous beansprout. While it is true that beansprouts are one of the most commonly-used ingredients in China, they are normally regarded as an everyday, homely type of food, which one would not expect to find on the menu of a restaurant, however humble.

◆

450 g/1 lb fresh beansprouts
1–2 spring onions, finely shredded
2.5 ml/½ tsp salt
5 ml/1 tsp sugar
15 ml/1 tbsp light soy sauce
10 ml/2 tsp sesame seed oil

◆

1 Wash and rinse the beansprouts in cold water, discarding the husks and other bits and pieces that float to the surface. Drain and shake off any excess water.
2 Cook the beansprouts on HIGH for 1 minute, stirring once. Rinse in cold water until cool. Drain well.
3 Place the sprouts in a serving bowl or deep dish, add the spring onions, salt, sugar and soy sauce, and mix well. Leave to stand for 10 minutes or so.
4 Sprinkle the salad with sesame seed oil and toss once more just before serving.
Note A little finely shredded fresh red chilli, cooked ham or carrot can be added as garnish to give this salad extra colour and flavour.

KIDNEY AND CELERY SALAD

In China the celery would be blanched or par-boiled before serving, but I do not think it is necessary to do so in the West.

◆

10 g/¼ oz wood ears (black fungus)
1 small head celery
5 ml/1 tsp salt
1 pair pig's kidneys (about 225 g/8 oz)
2 slices ginger root, peeled and thinly shredded
Sauce
15 ml/1 tbsp Shao Hsing rice wine or dry sherry
15 ml/1 tbsp light soy sauce
15 ml/1 tbsp vinegar
10 ml/2 tsp sesame seed oil

◆

1 Soak the wood ears in warm water for 25–30 minutes.

2 Discard the leaves and tough outer stalks of the celery. Cut the remaining stalks into thin slices diagonally, mix with the salt and leave to stand for 10 minutes or so.

3 Split each kidney in half lengthways, discarding the fat and tough white parts in the middle. Cut the kidneys into thin slices, then rinse in cold water until the water runs clear. Drain, place in a casserole and cover with boiling water. Cook on HIGH for 1 minute, then quickly remove the kidneys and run cold water over them for a few seconds. Drain.

4 Rinse the wood ears and remove any hard bits before cutting them into small pieces. Cook on HIGH for 2 minutes, stirring once.

5 To serve, place the wood ears and kidneys on top of the celery; garnish with the ginger shreds. Mix the sauce ingredients together and pour evenly over the salad. Toss well just before serving.

MIXED VEGETABLE SALAD WITH SPICY DRESSING

Chinese cabbage (bok choy), also known as Chinese leaves, has pale green leaves and long white stems with a crunchy texture. When unavailable, use celery, cabbage or Webb's lettuce instead.

◆

1 small head Chinese leaves
1 small green pepper, cored and seeded
1 small red pepper, cored and seeded
5 ml/1 tsp salt
2.5 ml/½ tsp Sichuan peppercorns, crushed
15 ml/1 tbsp sesame seed oil
1–2 spring onions, finely chopped
15 ml/1 tbsp light soy sauce
5 ml/1 tsp chilli oil or sauce (optional)

◆

1 Separate the Chinese leaves, discarding the tough outer ones; wash and dry thoroughly, then cut each leaf into large slices and place in a large serving bowl.

2 Thinly shred the green and red peppers, place them on top of the cabbage, then sprinkle evenly with the salt and pepper.

3 Heat the sesame seed oil in a small jug on HIGH for 30 seconds, add the spring onions and soy sauce, then stir and cook for 15 seconds.

4 Add the sauce to the salad and mix well. Leave it to stand for 15–20 minutes before serving. (If using chilli oil or chilli sauce as part of the dressing, it must be added to the salad *just* before serving.)

GREEN BEANS AND RED PEPPER SALAD

Choose young, fresh green beans, also known as French beans or dwarf beans, for this dish.

◆

225 g/8 oz French beans
1 medium red pepper, cored and seeded
5 ml/1 tsp salt
5 ml/1 tsp finely chopped ginger root
and/or 5 ml/1 tsp finely chopped red or green chilli
5 ml/1 tsp sugar
15 ml/1 tbsp light soy sauce
10 ml/2 tsp sesame seed oil

◆

1 Wash the beans, top and tail them, then snap each bean in half; very fine dwarf beans can be left whole.
2 Cook the beans on HIGH for 1 minute, then rinse them in cold water until cool. Drain and transfer to a serving dish.
3 Thinly shred the red pepper and add to the beans with the salt, ginger and/or chilli, sugar, soy sauce and oil. Mix well and toss again just before serving.

Left: Green Beans and Red Pepper Salad; *centre:* King Prawns with Sweet and Sour Sauce
(page 28); *right:* Shanghai Soya Duck (page 24)

KING PRAWNS WITH SWEET AND SOUR SAUCE

Use fresh prawns if possible, otherwise serve ready-cooked ones cold with this delicious sauce. When eating, you must not peel the prawn before putting it in your mouth; simply suck the sauce and extract the flesh from the shell at the same time. This is easily done if using chopsticks or fingers instead of fork and spoon.

675 g/1½ lb fresh whole king prawns
Sauce
30 ml/2 tbsp oil
2 spring onions, finely chopped
2 slices ginger root, peeled and finely chopped
30 ml/2 tbsp soy sauce
30 ml/2 tbsp Shao Hsing rice wine or dry sherry
30 ml/2 tbsp sugar
15 ml/1 tbsp vinegar
about 120 ml/4 fl oz stock or water
10 ml/2 tsp cornflour mixed with 15 ml/1 tbsp cold water
Garnish
lettuce leaves
fresh coriander or parsley

1 Preheat a browning dish according to the manufacturer's instructions.
2 Discard the heads and legs of the prawns, but keep the body shells on. Wash and dry thoroughly.
3 Sprinkle the oil in the hot dish, add the prawns and cook on HIGH for 2–3 minutes, turning once.
4 Add the spring onions, ginger root, soy sauce, wine, sugar, vinegar and stock or water. Cook for a further 1–2 minutes, then add the cornflour paste and stir vigorously for a few seconds. When all the prawns are coated with the glittering sauce, they are done.
5 Arrange the prawns neatly on a bed of lettuce leaves and garnish with fresh coriander or parsley. Serve hot or cold.

POACHED PRAWNS PEKING-STYLE

If fresh prawns are unavailable, use ready-cooked ones and serve cold; in this case all you need do is make the sauce.

225 g/8 oz uncooked prawns, peeled
300 ml/½ pt boiling water
5 ml/1 tsp finely chopped spring onions
5 ml/1 tsp finely chopped ginger root
Sauce
15 ml/1 tbsp sesame seed oil
30 ml/2 tbsp light soy sauce
5 ml/1 tsp sugar
15 ml/1 tbsp Shao Hsing rice wine or dry sherry
10 ml/2 tsp cornflour mixed with 15 ml/1 tbsp water

1 Thaw the prawns, if frozen, and pat dry with paper towels. Cut each in half lengthways.
2 Cook the prawns in boiling water on HIGH for 1 minute, then scoop them out with a strainer and plunge into a bowl of cold water for a few seconds. Drain well before placing the prawns on a serving dish. Garnish with the spring onions and ginger root.
3 Heat the oil in a small jug on HIGH for 30 seconds; add the soy sauce, sugar and wine, and cook for 10–15 seconds to dissolve the sugar. Mix in the cornflour paste and cook for a further 10 seconds. Stir the sauce well and pour evenly all over the prawns. Toss just before serving.

SICHUAN BON-BON CHICKEN

This popular dish from Sichuan is also known as 'Bang-Bang Chicken' in some restaurants because the meat is tenderized by banging it with a stick (bon in Chinese).

◆

225 g/8 oz chicken breast meat, boned and skinned
50 ml/2 fl oz water
1 lettuce heart
Sauce
30 ml/2 tbsp stock or water
5 ml/1 tsp sugar
30 ml/2 tbsp soy sauce
5 ml/1 tsp chilli oil
15 ml/1 tbsp sesame paste, or peanut butter creamed
with a little sesame seed oil

◆

1 Place the chicken in a small dish and cover with water. Cover and cook on HIGH for 4–5 minutes, or until just cooked. Remove the chicken and soak it in cold water for 10–15 minutes to cool; drain and pat dry. Brush with sesame seed oil and leave to dry for another 10–15 minutes.
2 Cut the lettuce leaves into shreds and place them on a serving dish.
3 Pound the chicken with a rolling pin to loosen the meat, then tear it into shreds with your fingers and place on top of the lettuce.
4 Mix all the sauce ingredients together and pour evenly over the chicken. Toss at the table just before serving.

SOY-BRAISED CHICKEN

This is a Cantonese recipe which can be prepared and cooked well in advance and served cold, so it is ideal for buffet-style parties.

◆

1.5 kg/3–3½ lb fresh chicken
15 ml/1 tbsp ground Sichuan peppercorns
30 ml/2 tbsp finely minced ginger root
45 ml/3 tbsp dark soy sauce
30 ml/2 tbsp light soy sauce
45 ml/3 tbsp Shao Hsing rice wine or dry sherry
30 ml/2 tbsp brown sugar
120 ml/4 fl oz stock or water
lettuce leaves to garnish

◆

1 Clean and dry the chicken, then rub both inside and out with the ground peppercorns and minced ginger root (dried ginger powder should *not* be used).
2 Mix the soy sauce, wine and sugar together, transfer to a strong freezer bag, add the chicken and marinate for at least 3–4 hours (longer if possible), turning it over every 30 minutes or so.
3 Tip the chicken and marinade into a large casserole, add the stock or water and bring to the boil on HIGH (4–5 minutes). Cover with a vented lid and cook on HIGH for 20–25 minutes, turning once or twice and being careful not to break the skin.
4 Remove from the oven and allow the chicken and sauce to cool for at least 1–2 hours before removing from the casserole to cool down further.
5 Chop the chicken into bite-size pieces (see p.8) and arrange them neatly on a bed of lettuce leaves; pour over a little of the sauce. To add more colour you can garnish the edge of the plate with cucumber and tomato slices. The remaining sauce may be stored in the refrigerator for several months, or can be used to make Braised Five-Spice Eggs (see p.30).

CHICKEN AND HAM SALAD WITH MUSTARD SAUCE

This is a well-known hors d'oeuvre from northern China. It is extremely simple to prepare.

◆

25 g/1 oz agar agar or isinglass
175 g/6 oz chicken breast meat, boned and skinned
115 g/4 oz cooked ham
½ cucumber
15 ml/1 tbsp English mustard powder
15 ml/1 tbsp light soy sauce
15 ml/1 tbsp vinegar
10 ml/2 tsp sesame seed oil

◆

1 Soak the agar agar in warm water for 25–30 minutes, until soft.
2 Place the chicken in a small dish with about 30 ml/2 tbsp water. Cover and cook on HIGH for 3–4 minutes, or until just cooked.
3 Shred the chicken, ham and cucumber to the same size, keeping them in separate piles.
4 Drain and dry the agar agar, then cut into matchstick-size lengths. Spread out on a serving plate, then pile on the cucumber, chicken and ham in that order to make a pyramid shape.
5 Mix the mustard powder with a little cold water to form a thin paste and leave to mellow for about 30 minutes before blending it with the soy sauce, vinegar and oil. Pour the sauce evenly all over the salad, but do not mix until your guests have had time to admire the carefully arranged pattern.

BRAISED FIVE-SPICE EGGS

For the best result, use more than one of the sauces from Soy-Braised Chicken (p.29), Shanghai Soya Duck (p.24), Fragrant Pork (p.33), Soy-braised Beef (p.33) or Braised Tripe and Tongue (p.32).

◆

6 eggs
at least 600 ml/1 pt sauce (see above)
15–30 ml/1–2 tbsp soy sauce (optional)

◆

1 Hard-boil the eggs in water for 10 minutes on top of a conventional stove. Cool under cold water, then carefully peel off the shells.
2 Place the peeled eggs in a casserole with the sauce. Bring to the boil on HIGH and add a little water and soy sauce to cover the eggs completely, if necessary. Cover with a vented lid and cook on MEDIUM for 10–15 minutes.
3 Leave the eggs to cool in the sauce for 2–3 hours.
4 Drain the eggs for 30 minutes or so, then cut them into quarters or thin slices. Arrange on a plate with garnishes or as one of several hors d'oeuvres.
Note To save time, you can cook this dish with one of the recipes mentioned above: simply add the peeled, hard-boiled eggs just before the last stage of cooking.

Top: Beansprout Salad (page 24); *bottom:* Chicken and Ham Salad with Mustard Sauce

CRYSTAL-BOILED PORK WITH CRUSHED GARLIC SAUCE

Another famous dish from Shanghai which is very easy to make.

◆

900 g/2 lb leg of pork, boned but not skinned
Sauce
2 cloves garlic, crushed and finely chopped
2 spring onions, finely chopped
5 ml/1 tsp finely chopped ginger root
5 ml/1 tsp sugar
60 ml/4 tbsp light soy sauce
10 ml/2 tsp sesame seed oil or 15 ml/1 tbsp chilli oil

◆

1 Place the pork in one piece, tied together with string if necessary, in a casserole. Add about 2 l/3½ pt boiling water, cover with a vented lid and bring back to the boil on HIGH (about 2–3 minutes). Skim off any scum, then cook on MEDIUM for 15–20 minutes.
2 Remove from the oven but leave the pork in the water for at least 2–3 hours before removing it to cool with the skin side up for 3–4 hours.
3 Mix all the sauce ingredients together.
4 To preserve the flavour and moist texture, do not cut the meat until just before serving. When ready to do so, cut off the skin, leaving only a thin layer of fat on top like a ham joint. Cut the meat into small, thin slices across the grain and arrange them neatly in rows on a plate. Pour the sauce evenly all over the pork.

BRAISED TRIPE AND TONGUE

You can use the stomach and tongue of ox, lamb or pig for this recipe, and you do not have to use both tripe and tongue at the same time; they can be cooked on separate occasions.

◆

900 g/2 lb tripe and/or tongue
30 ml/2 tbsp oil
2 spring onions
2–3 small pieces ginger root
4 star anise or 5 ml/1 tsp aniseed
3 sticks cinnamon
10 ml/2 tsp Sichuan peppercorns
5–6 cloves
15 ml/1 tbsp brown sugar
120 ml/4 fl oz Shao Hsing rice wine or dry sherry
5 ml/1 tsp salt
75 ml/5 tbsp soy sauce
600 ml/1 pt stock
sesame seed oil (optional)
finely chopped spring onions

◆

1 Thaw tripe, if necessary, and pat dry.
2 Preheat a browning dish according to the manufacturer's instructions – usually about 8 minutes. Sprinkle in the oil and lightly brown the tripe on both sides.
3 Transfer the tripe to a casserole, add all the other ingredients and bring to the boil on HIGH.
4 Cover with a vented lid and cook on LOW for 45–50 minutes. Leave to stand for at least 30 minutes, or better still, leave the tripe and/or tongue to cool in the sauce for 2–3 hours. The sauce can be strained and re-used; it will keep for many weeks in the refrigerator in an airtight container.
5 Cut the tripe and tongue into thin slices. Sprinkle with the sesame seed oil and spring onions just before serving.
Note Any leftovers may be stored in an airtight container in the refrigerator for 4–5 days.

FRAGRANT PORK

In China belly pork is known as 'five-flower meat' because when viewed in cross-section, the alternative layers of lean meat and fat form a pretty pink and white pattern.

◆

675 g/1½ lb belly pork
2 spring onions
2–3 small pieces ginger root
5 ml/1 tsp salt
4 star anise or 5 ml/1 tsp aniseed
3 sticks cinnamon
1 dried tangerine peel
8 cloves
85 g/3 oz rock candy or crystal sugar
175 ml/6 fl oz Shao Hsing rice wine or dry sherry
75 ml/5 tbsp soy sauce
lettuce leaves to garnish

◆

1 Cut the pork into large chunks measuring about 15 × 7.5 × 5 cm/6 × 3 × 2 in.
2 Place the meat in a large casserole with all the other ingredients and cover with boiling water. Bring back to the boil on HIGH (2–3 minutes). Cover with a vented lid and cook on MEDIUM for 45–50 minutes.
3 Remove the meat from the oven but leave to stand in the sauce for at least 30 minutes – longer if possible.
4 Remove the meat from the sauce, cut it into thin slices (rather like rashers of bacon), and serve it on a bed of lettuce. The sauce can be stored and re-used for cooking other meat, chicken or eggs.

SOY-BRAISED BEEF

This is a Muslim recipe from northern China; mutton or lamb can be cooked by the same method.

◆

675–900 g/1½–2 lb braising steak or shin of beef
2–3 spring onions
3–4 slices ginger root
45–60 ml/3–4 tbsp Shao Hsing rice wine or dry sherry
30–45 ml/2–3 tbsp brandy
5 ml/1 tsp salt
15 ml/1 tbsp sugar
5 ml/1 tsp five-spice powder
60–75 ml/4–5 tbsp soy sauce
Garnish
5 ml/1 tsp sesame seed oil (optional)
finely chopped spring onions

◆

1 Place the beef in a casserole with the spring onions and ginger root; add the wine, brandy and about 120 ml/4 fl oz boiling water. Bring to the boil on HIGH, skim off the scum, then cover with a vented lid and cook on LOW for 25–30 minutes.
2 Add the salt, sugar, five-spice powder and soy sauce; stir and cook on MEDIUM for 25–30 minutes more. Leave to stand for 30–45 minutes before removing the meat from the sauce to cool.
3 Thinly slice the beef just before serving, and sprinkle with the sesame seed oil and spring onions.

Left: Fragrant Pork (page 33), Poached Prawns Peking-style (page 28), and Soy-braised
Chicken (page 29); *right:* Mixed Vegetable Salad with Spicy Dressing (page 25)

ASSORTED HORS D'OEUVRES

Instead of serving a number of cold starters separately for the hors d'oeuvre course, it is more interesting to arrange the various items either in neat rows or a pattern on a large dish, in the style of *crudités*. Garnish with cucumber, tomatoes, radishes, lemons or fresh coriander to stimulate the eye as well as the appetite.

The complexity of assorted hors d'oeuvres should reflect the splendour of what is to follow, but it is usual to serve a minimum of four different items. These should consist of three 'meats' (fish, poultry and meat) and a vegetable. A selection of Poached Prawns, Soy-Braised Chicken, Fragrant Pork and Beansprout Salad would fit the bill, but if you serve more remember not to have more than one dish based on the same type of food – for instance, do not include both Fragrant Pork *and* Crystal-Boiled Pork, nor Poached Prawns with King Prawns on the same dish. The ingredients should be chosen for their harmonious contrast and balance in colour, aroma, flavour and texture.

VEGETABLES

SINCE CHINA HAS ALWAYS BEEN *an agricultural country – more than 80 per cent of the population still live and work on the land – it is only natural that vegetables should assume the predominant role in the people's daily diet.*

Vegetarianism has a long history in China. Traditionally the Chinese have always been highly aware of, indeed one can almost say obsessed by, the link between food and health. As early as the Zhou dynasty (c. 1028–221 BC), the Chinese had already discovered that all the essentials of a balanced diet were to be found in vegetables; in modern terms, these are vitamins, protein, fats, carbohydrates and mineral salts. Naturally the amounts vary in different vegetables, but in no other type of food are they more readily assimilated.

The Chinese have perfected the cooking of vegetables to a fine art, with preparation almost always kept light and simple. Obviously different types of vegetables should be treated differently; some require long cooking, while others may need to be cooked with more than one ingredient in order to gain a 'cross-blending' of flavours, and contrast in textures and colours.

In stir-fries all the ingredients are thinly sliced and shredded, then tossed and stirred in a little hot oil over a high heat for a very short time. This ensures flavour and texture retention.

Surely, I hear you cry, stir-frying should be done in a wok, not in a microwave oven! That was exactly what I used to believe until I actually cooked a vegetable dish by microwave. To my amazement, the food tasted truly delicious with a delicate flavour, bright colour and crisp texture, just like a Chinese stir-fried dish. As far as I am concerned, the only difference between a 'microwave stir-fry' and a 'wok stir-fry' is that you need to use far less oil in a microwave; this may well be a bonus factor for those who think the Chinese use a little too much oil in their cooking.

Top: Braised Chinese Broccoli; *centre:* Braised Aubergines (page 39); *bottom:* Stir-fried
Beansprouts

STIR-FRIED BEANSPROUTS

Only fresh beansprouts should be used, as canned beansprouts lack crispness and flavour.

◆

400 g/14 oz fresh beansprouts
1–2 spring onions, thinly shredded
30 ml/2 tbsp vegetable oil
5 ml/1 tsp salt
2.5 ml/½ tsp sugar
5 ml/1 tsp sesame seed oil (optional)

◆

1 Wash and rinse the beansprouts in cold water, discarding any husks and other bits that float to the surface.
2 Cut the spring onions into short lengths.
3 Heat the oil with the spring onions on HIGH for 1 minute, then add the sprouts and toss well. Cook on HIGH for 2–3 minutes, stirring frequently.
4 Add the salt, sugar and sesame oil (if using), and cook for 1 more minute, stirring after 30 seconds or so. (Do not overcook, or the sprouts will become soggy.) Serve hot or cold.

BRAISED AUBERGINES

Choose the slender, purple variety of aubergine rather than the large round kind for this recipe, which comes from Shanghai in eastern China.

◆

450 g/1 lb aubergines
30 ml/2 tbsp stock or water
2 cloves garlic, crushed
5 ml/1 tsp finely chopped ginger root
15 ml/1 tbsp soy sauce
30 ml/2 tbsp Hoi Sin sauce, or 15 ml/1 tbsp crushed
yellow bean paste mixed with 10 ml/2 tsp sugar
5 ml/1 tsp cornflour mixed with 15 ml/1 tbsp water
5 ml/1 tsp sesame seed oil

◆

1 Remove the stems from the aubergines, but do not peel. Cut into diagonal slices about 2.5 cm/1 in thick.
2 Cook the aubergines with stock or water, garlic and ginger on HIGH for 4–6 minutes, stirring once or twice.
3 Add the soy sauce and bean paste, mix well and cook on MEDIUM for about 2 minutes, stirring once or twice.
4 Thicken the stock with the cornflour paste, add the sesame seed oil and mix well. Serve hot or cold.

'BUDDHAS' DELIGHT' – EIGHT TREASURES OF CHINESE VEGETABLES

The original recipe calls for eighteen different ingredients to represent the eighteen Buddhas (Luoham in Chinese). Later this was reduced to eight, usually consisting half and half of dried and fresh vegetables.

◆

15 g/½ oz dried bean curd skin sticks
15 g/½ oz golden needles (dried tiger-lily buds)
15 g/½ oz wood ears (black fungus)
15 g/½ oz dried Chinese mushrooms
115 g/4 oz straw or button mushrooms
115 g/4 oz mange-tout
115 g/4 oz bamboo shoots
115 g/4 oz young carrots
30–45 ml/2–3 tbsp vegetable oil
5 ml/1 tsp salt
5 ml/1 tsp sugar
15 ml/1 tbsp light soy sauce
5 ml/1 tsp cornflour mixed with 15 ml/1 tbsp cold water
5 ml/1 tsp sesame seed oil

◆

1 Soak the dried bean curd sticks overnight in cold water (at least 10–12 hours), or in hot water for 3–4 hours.
2 Soak the golden needles and wood ears in warm water for 25–30 minutes.
3 Soak the dried mushrooms in warm water for 20–25 minutes.
4 Drain the bean curd sticks and cut into short lengths.
5 Drain the golden needles and cut in half.
6 Rinse the wood ears discarding any hard bits. Squeeze dry; leave whole if small, otherwise cut the large ones into 3 or 4 pieces.
7 Drain the mushrooms and chop to the same size as the golden needles.
8 Cut the straw or button mushrooms in half if large, otherwise leave whole.

9 Top and tail the mange-tout; snap in half if large, but leave whole if small.
10 Cut the bamboo shoots and carrots into thin slices about the size of an oblong postage stamp.
11 Heat about half the oil on HIGH for 1 minute, then fry the bean curd, mange-tout and carrots for 2–3 minutes, stirring once or twice.
12 Add the rest of the vegetables with the salt, sugar, soy sauce, cornflour paste and remaining oil. Mix well and cook on HIGH for 2–3 minutes, stirring frequently. Sprinkle with sesame seed oil and serve hot or cold.

BRAISED BRUSSELS SPROUTS

Choose sprouts of the same size, if possible, otherwise halve or quarter large ones.

◆

450 g/1 lb Brussels sprouts
30 ml/2 tbsp vegetable oil
30 ml/2 tbsp stock or water
5 ml/1 tsp salt
5 ml/1 tsp sugar
10 ml/2 tsp light soy sauce

◆

1 Wash the sprouts, discard all the tough outer leaves, and trim the stems. Make a cross-cut through the base of each with a sharp knife.
2 Heat the oil on HIGH for 1 minute, then add the sprouts and stock or water. Stir and cook on HIGH for 4–6 minutes (the time depends on the size of the sprouts). Stir frequently.
3 Add the salt, sugar and soy sauce, mix well and cook on MEDIUM for 40–50 seconds, stirring once. Serve hot.

QUICK-FRY OF 'FOUR PRECIOUS VEGETABLES'

The 'four precious vegetables' are chosen for their harmonious contrast in colour and texture. They can be varied with seasonal availability, so the bamboo shoots, for instance, can be replaced by courgettes or cauliflower, and the mange-tout can be replaced with lettuce heart or asparagus.

5–6 dried Chinese mushrooms
225 g/8 oz canned bamboo shoots
115 g/4 oz mange-tout
225 g/8 oz young carrots
30 ml/2 tbsp vegetable oil
5 ml/1 tsp salt
2.5 ml/½ tsp sugar
15 ml/1 tbsp light soy sauce
a few drops of sesame seed oil

1 Soak the mushrooms in warm water for 20–25 minutes.
2 Drain the bamboo shoots and slice thinly.
3 Wash the mange-tout, then top and tail. Leave whole if small, otherwise snap in half.
4 Scrub the carrots and thinly slice diagonally.
5 Squeeze the mushrooms dry, discard the hard stalks, and slice thinly.
6 Heat the oil on HIGH for about 1 minute, then cook the carrots and mange-tout on HIGH for 2–3 minutes, stirring once or twice.
7 Add the bamboo shoots and mushrooms and cook for 2 more minutes.
8 Add the salt and sugar, stir and cook for 1 more minute.
9 Add the soy sauce and sesame seed oil, mix well and serve hot or cold.

FU-YUNG BEAN CURD

In most Chinese restaurants, fu-yung *means omelette, but strictly speaking, it really means scrambled egg-whites with a creamy texture.*

1 lettuce heart
50 ml/2 fl oz stock
5 ml/1 tsp salt
2 cakes bean curd
4 egg whites, lightly beaten
15 ml/1 tbsp cornflour mixed with 30 ml/2 tbsp milk or water
5 ml/1 tsp finely chopped spring onions
5 ml/1 tsp finely chopped ginger root
5 ml/1 tsp sesame seed oil

1 Wash and separate the lettuce leaves.
2 Place the stock in a deep round dish or glass bowl and bring to a rolling boil on HIGH (1–2 minutes). Add half the salt and blanch the lettuce leaves for 1–2 minutes, stirring once or twice. Remove with a slotted spoon and arrange on a serving dish.
3 Cut the bean curd into thin shreds, and cook in the stock on HIGH for 2–3 minutes, stirring gently once or twice.
4 Mix the egg whites with the cornflour paste, spring onions, ginger root and remaining salt. Pour the mixture over the bean curd and cook on MEDIUM for 2–3 minutes, or until just set, stirring once or twice.
5 Sprinkle the *fu-yung* with the sesame seed oil and serve on the bed of lettuce leaves.

BEAN CURD WITH SPINACH

Try to buy your spinach from an Oriental food store; it is usually sold in small bundles with the bright red roots still attached and these add extra colour to the dish.

◆

275 g/10 oz fresh spinach
2 cakes bean curd
30 ml/2 tbsp vegetable oil
1 clove garlic, crushed
5 ml/1 tsp salt
2.5 ml/½ tsp sugar
15 ml/1 tbsp soy sauce
a few drops of sesame seed oil

◆

1 Preheat a browning dish according to the manufacturer's instructions – usually about 8 minutes.
2 Wash the spinach thoroughly and shake off as much water as possible.
3 Cut each cake of bean curd into about 8–10 pieces.
4 Heat the oil in the hot browning dish with the garlic. Add the bean curd and fry on HIGH for 2–3 minutes, turning gently once or twice. Remove and set aside.
5 Cook the spinach on HIGH for about 2 minutes, or until the leaves are limp. Add the bean curd, salt, sugar and soy sauce; stir very gently to combine, then cook for another 2 minutes, stirring once or twice during cooking.
6 Add the sesame seed oil and serve hot.

MIXED VEGETABLES

The Chinese never mix ingredients indiscriminately; items are carefully selected with the aim of achieving a harmonious balance of colour, aroma, flavour and texture. This recipe demonstrates the balance beautifully.

◆

25 g/1 oz wood ears (black fungus)
115 g/4 oz broccoli florets
115 g/4 oz straw mushrooms or oyster mushrooms
115 g/4 oz baby corn, fresh or canned
115 g/4 oz courgettes
1 small green or red pepper, cored and seeded
30 ml/2 tbsp vegetable oil
5 ml/1 tsp salt
5 ml/1 tsp sugar
15 ml/1 tbsp light soy sauce
a few drops of sesame seed oil (optional)

◆

1 Soak the wood ears in warm water for 20–25 minutes.
2 Prepare the other vegetables by cutting them into roughly uniform sizes. The mushrooms can be left whole, but if exceptionally large, halve or quarter them. Leave the baby corn whole if tiny, otherwise cut each one into 3 or 4 small diamond-shaped pieces.
3 Rinse the wood ears and discard the hard parts.
4 Heat the oil on HIGH for 1 minute, then add the broccoli, baby corn and courgettes; mix well and cook on HIGH for 3–4 minutes, stirring frequently.
5 Add the wood ears, mushrooms and peppers, followed by the salt, sugar and soy sauce. Toss and turn until well mixed, then cook on HIGH for 2 minutes.
6 Add the sesame seed oil (if using), and serve hot or cold.

Top: Mixed vegetables; *bottom:* Bean Curd with Spinach

BRAISED BEAN CURD

Traditionally served as the very last course of a big, rich Chinese banquet, this refreshing vegetarian dish offers a welcome relief to the jaded palate.

◆

3–4 dried Chinese mushrooms
or 50 g/2 oz fresh mushrooms
4 cakes bean curd
15–30 ml/1–2 tbsp vegetable oil
15 ml/1 tbsp Shao Hsing rice wine or dry sherry
2.5 ml/½ tsp salt
2.5 ml/½ tsp sugar
15 ml/1 tbsp light soy sauce
5 ml/1 tsp cornflour mixed with a little water
5 ml/1 tsp sesame seed oil

◆

1 Soak the dried mushrooms in warm water for 20–25 minutes. Squeeze dry and discard the hard stalks. Keep the water for use as stock.
2 Slice the bean curd into 5 mm/¼ in thick slices, then cut each slice into 6–8 pieces.
3 Heat the oil on HIGH for 1 minute, add the mushrooms, mix well and cook on HIGH for 1 minute.
4 Pour in about 120 ml/4 fl oz mushroom-soaking water or good stock, bring to the boil (about 2 minutes), then add the bean curd, wine, salt, sugar and soy sauce. Mix well and cook on HIGH for 2–3 minutes, stirring gently once or twice.
5 Pour the cornflour paste evenly over the bean curd, stir well and cook on MEDIUM for 30–40 seconds.
6 Sprinkle with the sesame seed oil to give a clear, light glaze. Serve immediately.

GREEN PEPPERS, TOMATOES AND ONIONS

Tomatoes are a fairly recent introduction to Chinese cooking and they give this colourful mixed vegetable dish quite a different flavour.

◆

1 large green pepper (about 225 g/8 oz)
1 large onion
225 g/8 oz firm tomatoes
15–30 ml/1–2 tbsp vegetable oil
5 ml/1 tsp salt
5 ml/1 tsp sugar
a few drops of sesame seed oil (optional)

◆

1 Wash, core and seed the green peppers, then cut them into small diamond-shaped pieces about the size of a postage stamp.
2 Cut the onions and tomatoes into roughly uniform pieces.
3 Heat the oil on HIGH for about 1 minute. Add the onions and cook on HIGH for 2 minutes, stirring once or twice.
4 Add the green peppers and cook on HIGH for 2–3 minutes, stirring frequently.
5 Stir in the tomatoes with the salt and sugar, mix well and cook for 1 minute more on HIGH.
6 Sprinkle with the sesame oil (if using) and serve hot or cold.

BRAISED 'TWO WINTERS'

This recipe takes its name from the two main ingredients: winter bamboo shoots and winter mushrooms. There are several varieties of bamboo shoot, which vary in size, texture and season. The best are usually dug just before they appear above the ground during the winter, and these are known as winter bamboo shoots. They are quite small, not much bigger than pine cones, and the ivory-coloured flesh is tender and delicious. Winter mushrooms are better known in the West as dried Chinese mushrooms.

◆

8–10 dried Chinese mushrooms
400 g/14 oz winter bamboo shoots
15 ml/1 tbsp vegetable oil
30 ml/2 tbsp light soy sauce
5 ml/1 tsp sugar
5 ml/1 tsp cornflour
a few drops of sesame seed oil

◆

1 Select small mushrooms of a uniform size and soak in warm water for 20–25 minutes; squeeze dry and discard the hard stalks, but keep the water for later use.
2 Slice the bamboo shoots into roughly the same size as the mushrooms.
3 Cook the mushrooms and bamboo shoots with the oil, soy sauce and sugar on HIGH for 3–4 minutes, stirring frequently.
4 Mix the cornflour with a little of the mushroom water and stir into the vegetables; cook for 1 minute more on MEDIUM, stirring once or twice.
5 Sprinkle with sesame seed oil and serve hot or cold.

VEGETARIAN CASSEROLE

Make this colourful, healthy casserole for your vegetarian friends, and you may be converted yourself.

◆

6–8 dried Chinese mushrooms
2 cakes bean curd
175 g/6 oz French beans or mange-tout
115 g/4 oz bamboo shoots or baby corn
115 g/4 oz carrots
30–45 ml/2–3 tbsp vegetable oil
5 ml/1 tsp salt
5 ml/1 tsp sugar
15 ml/1 tbsp light soy sauce
5 ml/1 tsp cornflour
5 ml/1 tsp sesame seed oil (optional)

◆

1 Soak the mushrooms in warm water for 20–25 minutes.
2 Cut the bean curd into about 12 pieces.
3 Top and tail the French beans or mange-tout. Cut the rest of the vegetables into thin slices or diamond-shaped chunks.
4 Squeeze the mushrooms dry, discard the hard stalks and cut into thin slices. Retain the mushroom water.
5 Heat the oil in a casserole on HIGH for 1 minute and cook the bean curd for 2 minutes, stirring gently once or twice.
6 Add the rest of the vegetables with salt, sugar and soy sauce. Cook for 2–3 minutes more, stirring frequently.
7 Mix the cornflour with about 30 ml/2 tbsp of the mushroom water, add to the casserole and mix well. Cover with a vented lid and cook on MEDIUM for 2–3 minutes.
8 Add the sesame seed oil and serve hot.

ASPARAGUS TIPS CHINESE-STYLE

*Choose the freshest asparagus available –
ideally, home-grown, so you can pick them just
before cooking them. The dark green and slender
variety has more flavour than the pale,
overgrown fat ones.*

◆

400 g/14 oz asparagus
15 ml/1 tbsp vegetable oil
2.5 ml/½ tsp salt
2.5 ml/½ tsp sugar
15 ml/1 tbsp oyster sauce or 5 ml/1 tsp light soy sauce

◆

1 Wash the asparagus and discard the
tough ends of the stalks. Cut the tender
part of the shoots into 2.5 cm/1 in lengths,
using the roll-cutting method: make a
diagonal slice through the stalk, then roll it
half a turn and slice again, so that you end
up with diamond-shaped slices.
2 Heat the oil on HIGH for 1 minute, add
the asparagus, stir and shake, and cook on
HIGH for 3–4 minutes, stirring frequently.
3 Add the salt, sugar and sauce, mix well
and cook for another 30–40 seconds. Serve
hot or cold.

Left: Braised 'Two Winters' (page 45); *centre below:* Green Peppers, Tomatoes and Onions
(page 44); *top right:* Asparagus Tips Chinese-style

STIR-FRIED GREEN CABBAGE

In Britain the cabbage season lasts almost all year round; from March to the end of summer there are oval-shaped spring greens, from September to February round, firm-hearted winter cabbages are available, and in between these two seasons there are enough early and late varieties to ensure a ready supply.

◆

675 g/1½ lb young green cabbage
30 ml/2 tbsp vegetable oil
5 ml/1 tsp finely chopped ginger root
5 ml/1 tsp salt
2.5 ml/½ tsp sugar
10 ml/2 tsp light soy sauce
5 ml/1 tsp sesame seed oil (optional)

◆

1 Discard any tough, outer cabbage leaves, then wash the rest in cold water. Drain and cut into thin strips like sauerkraut or coleslaw.

2 Heat the oil with the ginger on HIGH for 1 minute, then add the cabbage and toss well. Cook on HIGH for 4–5 minutes, stirring frequently during cooking.

3 Add the salt, sugar and soy sauce and mix well. Cook on HIGH for 30–40 seconds more, or until the cabbage is done. Do not overcook, or the cabbage will lose its crispness, as well as much of its vitamin content.

4 Add the sesame seed oil and toss once more just before serving.

STIR-FRIED GREEN BEANS

All sorts of beans – French, dwarf, runner, or mange-tout – can be stir-fried provided they are young and tender. Old, wilted beans are usually stringy and tasteless, so avoid buying them.

◆

275 g/10 oz green beans
15 ml/1 tbsp stock or water
5 ml/1 tsp salt
2.5 ml/½ tsp sugar
10 ml/2 tsp light soy sauce
5 ml/1 tsp finely chopped chives
5 ml/1 tsp sesame seed oil or salad oil

◆

1 Wash the beans in cold water, and top and tail them, stringing them if necessary. Slender dwarf beans and small mange-tout can be left whole; larger ones should be snapped in half, and runner beans may need to be sliced with a knife.

2 Cook the beans with the stock or water on HIGH for 4–6 minutes, stirring two or three times during cooking. Add the salt, sugar and soy sauce, mix well, then cook for another 30 seconds or so. (The time depends on the age and size of the beans.)

3 Add the chives and sesame oil, and toss well. Serve hot or cold.

BRAISED CHINESE LEAVES WITH MUSHROOMS

There are two varieties of Chinese leaves: one type is the same shape as cos lettuce, but has pale green, curly leaves with long white stems; the other type has a shorter, fatter head with pale yellow leaves. Both varieties will keep fresh for a long time and retain their crunchy texture even after lengthy cooking.

◆

1 head Chinese leaves (about 400 g/14 oz)
350 g/12 oz canned straw mushrooms, or 225 g/8 oz
fresh button mushrooms
50 ml/2 fl oz stock or water
5 ml/1 tsp sugar
7.5 ml/1½ tsp salt
10 ml/2 tsp cornflour mixed with 15 ml/1 tbsp milk
5 ml/1 tsp sesame seed oil

◆

1 Separate the leaves and cut each in half lengthways.
2 Drain the mushrooms, if using canned; trim, but do not peel fresh ones.
3 Cook the leaves with the stock or water on HIGH for 3–4 minutes, stirring once or twice.
4 Add the sugar and 5 ml/1 tsp of the salt. Cook for another minute or so, then remove the leaves with a slotted spoon and arrange neatly on one side of a serving dish.
5 Add the mushrooms to the stock with the remaining salt and cook on HIGH for 2–3 minutes.
6 Thicken the stock with the cornflour paste, stirring until smooth. Remove the mushrooms with a slotted spoon and place them next to the leaves on the serving plate. Pour the creamy sauce evenly over the vegetables. Sprinkle with the sesame seed oil and serve hot.

TOMATO AND EGG SCRAMBLE

For this colourful dish you should use firm, green tomatoes. They can be hard to come by, unless you grow your own, but try to buy the firmest and most under-ripe ones available. Alternatively, other vegetables, such as cucumber, green peppers or peas, can be substituted for the tomatoes.

◆

275 g/10 oz firm, green tomatoes
4–5 eggs
5 ml/1 tsp salt
2 spring onions, finely chopped
15 ml/1 tbsp vegetable oil

◆

1 Cut the tomatoes into small slices.
2 Beat the eggs with a pinch of salt and about a third of the chopped spring onion.
3 Place the eggs and oil in an ovenproof dish or glass bowl and cook on HIGH for 1 minute, stirring well after 30 seconds.
4 Add the tomatoes and the remaining salt; continue cooking for 1–1½ minutes, or until the eggs are just cooked, stirring frequently. Add the remaining spring onion and serve hot.

QUICK-BRAISED LETTUCE HEART

It is best to use a crisp lettuce, such as cos, Webb's or iceberg for this recipe. If you use the floppy, soft variety, you will probably need to use two or three heads.

◆

1 large crisp lettuce
15–30 ml/1–2 tbsp stock
15 ml/1 tbsp vegetable oil
2.5 ml/½ tsp salt
15 ml/1 tbsp oyster sauce or 10 ml/2 tsp light soy sauce

◆

1 Discard the tough outer lettuce leaves and wash the tender heart in cold water. Shake off excess water and cut the heart in quarters lengthways, or in 6–8 segments if using a round variety.
2 Cook the lettuce heart with the stock on HIGH for 2–3 minutes, stirring once.
3 Meanwhile heat the oil with the salt and sauce until bubbling. Pour the mixture over the lettuce heart and toss well. Serve hot or cold.
Note: Make sure you do not overcook the lettuce or it will lose its crispness and bright green colour.

Left: Quick-fry of Four Precious Vegetables (page 41); *centre:* Quick-braised Lettuce Heart;
right: Steamed Cauliflower in Cream Sauce (page 53)

'THREE WHITES' IN CREAM SAUCE

The 'three whites' are Chinese leaves, asparagus and celery heart. Although slender, green asparagus was known in China as early as the Tang Dynasty (AD 618–907), the fat, white variety is a comparatively modern introduction from the West.

◆

1 small head Chinese leaves (about
225–275 g/8–10 oz)
225 g/8 oz fresh white asparagus
or 275 g/10 oz canned asparagus spears
1–2 celery hearts
50 ml/2 fl oz stock
5 ml/1 tsp salt
15 ml/1 tbsp vegetable oil
5 ml/1 tsp finely chopped spring onions
(white part only)
5 ml/1 tsp finely chopped ginger root
15 ml/1 tbsp cornflour mixed with 45 ml/3 tbsp milk or
water

◆

1 Cut the Chinese leaves lengthways into thin strips, discarding any discoloured outer leaves.
2 Trim off the tough ends of the asparagus; if using canned, simply drain off the water.
3 Cut the celery hearts lengthways into thin strips.
4 Cook the Chinese leaves with the stock and a little salt on HIGH for 2–3 minutes, stirring once or twice; remove with a pair of chopsticks or tongs and arrange the strips neatly in the centre of a serving dish.
5 Cook the asparagus in the same stock on HIGH for 3–4 minutes, stirring once or twice; remove and arrange them neatly on one side of the Chinese leaves. (If using canned asparagus, heat on MEDIUM for 1½-2 minutes.)
6 Cook the celery hearts on HIGH for 2–3 minutes, stirring once or twice, then remove with chopsticks or tongs, and arrange neatly on the other side of the Chinese leaves.
7 Add the oil, spring onions, ginger and remaining salt to the stock and bring to the boil on HIGH (1–1½ minutes), stirring once.
8 Mix in the cornflour paste and cook on MEDIUM for 40–50 seconds, stirring until smooth and creamy.
9 Pour the sauce evenly over the vegetables. Serve hot.

BRAISED CHINESE BROCCOLI

Chinese Broccoli (Brassica parachinensis) has long, pale green stalks with dark green leaves. Sometimes it has a sprig of bright yellow flower in the centre, which is very much prized by the Chinese.

400 g/14 oz Chinese broccoli
30–45 ml/2–3 tbsp stock or water
15 ml/1 tbsp vegetable oil
2.5 ml/½ tsp salt
2.5 ml/½ tsp sugar
15 ml/1 tbsp oyster sauce or light soy sauce

◆

1 Trim off the tough ends of the broccoli stems, and discard any discoloured and wilted leaves. Wash and cut the stalks into short lengths.
2 Cook the stalks with the stock or water on HIGH for 2–3 minutes, stirring once or twice.
3 Add the oil, salt, sugar and sauce; mix well and cook on HIGH for 1 more minute, stirring once. Serve hot.

CHINESE LEAVES AND BEAN CURD CASSEROLE

The deep-fried bean curd used in this recipe is sold in most Oriental food stores with about ten pieces in each 25 g/1 oz packet. Alternatively, make your own by dicing fresh bean curd and deep-frying it in very hot vegetable oil until puffed up and golden.

◆

15 g/½ oz wood ears (black fungus)
450 g/1 lb Chinese leaves
50 g/2 oz deep-fried bean curd
30 ml/2 tbsp vegetable oil
5 ml/1 tsp salt
5 ml/1 tsp sugar
15 ml/1 tbsp light soy sauce
30 ml/2 tbsp Shao Hsing rice wine or dry sherry
a few drops of sesame seed oil
fresh coriander to garnish

◆

1 Soak the wood ears in water for 25–30 minutes.
2 Separate the Chinese leaves, wash them and cut into small pieces.
3 Heat the oil in a casserole on HIGH for 1 minute, add the leaves and cook for 2–3 minutes, stirring once or twice.
4 Rinse the wood ears, discarding the hard parts.
5 Add the bean curd, wood ears, salt, sugar, soy sauce and wine; mix well and cook on HIGH for 2–3 minutes, stirring frequently.
6 Sprinkle with sesame seed oil and garnish with coriander leaves. Serve hot.

STEAMED CAULIFLOWER IN CREAM SAUCE

When choosing cauliflower, make sure the leaves that curl round the head are not withered; bright green leaves indicate that the cauliflower is freshly picked.

◆

1 medium-sized cauliflower (about 675 g/1½ lb)
15 ml/1 tbsp stock or water
15 ml/1 tbsp vegetable oil
5 ml/1 tsp salt
Sauce
50 ml/2 fl oz stock or water
15 ml/1 tbsp cornflour mixed with a little cold water
finely chopped spring onions or chives to garnish

◆

1 Wash the cauliflower, trim off the hard, discoloured root, and discard the tough outer leaves. Keep a few of the tender, pale green leaves, as they add colour and flavour to the dish. Cut the cauliflower into small florets, and the stalks into thin slices.
2 Cook the cauliflower with the stock or water on HIGH for 4–6 minutes, stirring frequently. Add the salt and oil, mix well and cook for 2 more minutes, stirring once or twice.
3 Make the sauce by heating the stock or water in a small jug on HIGH for 2–3 minutes; stir in the cornflour paste and cook on MEDIUM for 40–50 seconds, stirring until smooth.
4 Pour the sauce evenly over the cauliflower. Garnish with spring onions or chives and serve hot.

Top: Braised Chinese Leaves with Mushrooms (page 49); *centre:* Braised Brussels Sprouts
(page 40); *bottom:* Courgettes with Red Peppers

COURGETTES WITH RED PEPPERS

Do not peel the courgettes for this dish, if you want to retain the colour and vitamin content.

◆

450 g/1 lb courgettes
1 medium or 2 small red peppers
15 ml/1 tbsp vegetable oil
2.5 ml/½ tsp salt
5 ml/1 tsp sugar
5 ml/1 tsp light soy sauce

◆

1 Wash the courgettes and trim the ends. Split each courgette in half lengthways, then slice each half diagonally.
2 Wash, seed and core the red peppers, then cut them into diamond-shaped pieces roughly the same size as the courgettes.
3 Heat the oil on HIGH for 1 minute, add the courgettes, mix well and cook on HIGH for 2–3 minutes, stirring once or twice.
4 Add the red peppers with the salt, sugar and soy sauce, mix well and cook on HIGH for 2 more minutes, stirring once or twice. Serve hot or cold.

BRAISED BROCCOLI IN OYSTER SAUCE

As with cauliflower, broccoli is rather difficult to cook evenly in the microwave due to the different textures of the florets and stalks. It is therefore best to cook the florets and stalks separately. The Cantonese are particularly fond of the crunchy stalks, and oyster sauce seems to have made an ideal partner for this vegetable.

◆

450 g/1 lb fresh broccoli
30 ml/2 tbsp vegetable oil
2–3 small pieces ginger root, peeled
5 ml/1 tsp salt
2.5 ml/½ tsp sugar
30–45 ml/2–3 tbsp stock or water
30 ml/2 tbsp oyster sauce

◆

1 Cut the broccoli into florets; remove the rough skin from the stalks, and slice them diagonally.
2 Heat the oil with the ginger on HIGH for 1 minute, add the broccoli stalks, then stir and cook on HIGH for 2–3 minutes.
3 Add the florets with the salt and sugar; continue stirring and add the stock or water. Quick-braise on HIGH for 2–3 minutes, stirring frequently.
4 Add the oyster sauce, mix well and serve hot or cold.

FISH

THE CHINESE EAT FAR MORE *fish than meat in their daily diet, partly because of its abundance. This tendency is not merely confined to coastal regions; inland parts have plenty of freshwater fish from rivers, streams and lakes, while ponds double as reservoirs and fish farms.*

The most important factor to take into account when buying fish is freshness. I think it is not generally appreciated in the West that fish is much more perishable than meat or poultry; in China fish and shellfish are usually sold still alive, so freshness is guaranteed. In the West, efficient refrigeration on board modern fishing vessels keeps the catch reasonably fresh for a few days, and after it has been landed it continues its journey to the fishmonger's slab packed in ice. But, given the delay, it is unrealistic to expect the fish to keep fresh for more than a few hours after you have purchased it from the fishmonger, even if it is stored in your refrigerator. Deep-freezing is no solution, as it significantly affects the flavour and texture of fish: the flesh loses its springiness, and cooking only makes it dry, tough and tasteless.

Another important point to remember is that the flesh of most fish, particularly shellfish, is very delicate and will lose much of its flavour and texture if cooked too long.

SQUID-FLOWERS WITH GREEN PEPPERS

Seafood cooking is a Cantonese speciality, and this recipe reflects the local skill. Be careful not to overcook squid or it becomes as tough as rubber.

◆

450 g/1 lb squid
1 large green pepper, cored and seeded
30 ml/2 tbsp vegetable oil
1 clove garlic, crushed and finely chopped
5 ml/1 tsp finely chopped ginger root
1–2 spring onions, finely chopped
2.5 ml/½ tsp salt
10 ml/2 tsp vinegar
15 ml/1 tbsp Shao Hsing rice wine or dry sherry
15 ml/1 tbsp salted black bean sauce
a few drops of sesame seed oil
coriander leaves to garnish

◆

1 Prepare the squid by discarding the head, ink sac and transparent backbone; peel off the skin, then wash and dry. Cut open the squid, closely score the *inside* in a criss-cross pattern, then cut into pieces about the size of an oblong postage stamp. Blanch the pieces in boiling water for 30–40 seconds, or until they curl up and the criss-cross pattern opens out to resemble ears of corn. Rinse in cold water and drain.
2 Cut the green pepper into triangular pieces about the size of a postage stamp.
3 Heat the oil on HIGH for 1 minute; add the garlic, ginger and spring onions to flavour the oil for a few seconds, then stir in the peppers and squid. Cook on HIGH for 1½–2 minutes, stirring once or twice, then mix in the salt, vinegar, wine and black bean sauce. Continue cooking on HIGH for 1 minute more, stirring once.
4 Sprinkle the squid with sesame seed oil, garnish with coriander and serve hot.

Left: Seafood Casserole (page 60); *centre below:* Squid-flowers with Green Peppers; *right:*
Sichuan Prawns with Garlic and Chilli Sauce (page 61)

SEAFOOD CASSEROLE

Another speciality from Canton, this dish is a cross between bouillabaisse and paella, in which several different kinds of fish and/or shellfish are cooked together with vegetables.

◆

3–4 dried Chinese mushrooms
225 g/8 oz assorted shellfish, such as prawns, scallops, mussels, oysters or whelks (use only 2 different kinds at most)
450 g/1 lb assorted fish steaks or cutlets, such as cod, haddock, monkfish, whiting, salmon or eel (do not use more than 3 different kinds)
5 ml/1 tsp salt
1 egg white, lightly beaten
15 ml/1 tbsp cornflour mixed with a little water
50 g/2 oz lean pork
30–45 ml/2–3 tbsp vegetable oil
2–3 cakes bean curd
4–6 Chinese leaves or lettuce leaves
2–3 slices ginger root, peeled
2 spring onions, thinly shredded
30 ml/2 tbsp light soy sauce
2.5 ml/½ tsp sugar
30 ml/2 tbsp Shao Hsing rice wine or dry sherry
120 ml/4 fl oz stock or water
salt and freshly ground Sichuan pepper to taste
fresh coriander to garnish

◆

1 Soak the mushrooms in warm water.
2 Shell or peel the shellfish, as necessary, then wash and pat dry. Coat the fish with salt, egg white and cornflour.
3 Squeeze the mushrooms dry, discard the stalks and thinly shred these and the pork.
4 Heat the oil in a preheated browning dish while cutting each cake of bean curd into 6–8 pieces; cook on HIGH for 1–2 minutes, turning gently until golden. Remove and place in a casserole lined with Chinese leaves or lettuce.
5 Cook the fish steaks in the same oil on HIGH for 2–3 minutes, or until golden, turning gently once or twice; remove and

place on top of the bean curd in the casserole.
6 Add the shredded pork, mushrooms, ginger, spring onions, soy sauce, sugar, wine and stock to the casserole; mix well, cover with a vented lid and cook on HIGH for about 2 minutes.
7 Add the shellfish and cook on HIGH for 1–2 minutes, or until boiling, stirring very gently once or twice. Garnish with coriander leaves and serve hot.

EGG FU-YUNG WITH PRAWNS OR CRABMEAT

The delicate flavours of prawns and crab go very well with this dish of lightly-scrambled eggs.

◆

5–6 eggs
115 g/4 oz peeled prawns or flaked crabmeat
2.5 ml/½ tsp finely chopped ginger root
2 spring onions, finely chopped
5 ml/1 tsp salt
50 g/2 oz button mushrooms
30 ml/2 tbsp vegetable oil
15 ml/1 tbsp Shao Hsing rice wine or dry sherry
coriander leaves or parsley to garnish

◆

1 Lightly beat the eggs, then add the prawns or crabmeat, ginger root, about a third of the spring onions and a pinch of salt.
2 Cut the mushrooms into thin slices.
3 Heat the oil on HIGH for about 1 minute. Add the mushrooms and remaining spring onions and cook on HIGH for 40–50 seconds, stirring once.
4 Add the salt and wine and cook for 1 more minute.
5 Stir in the egg and prawn mixture, cook on HIGH for 1–2 minutes, or until set (not too hard), stirring once or twice. Serve hot garnished with coriander leaves or parsley.

SICHUAN PRAWNS WITH GARLIC AND CHILLI SAUCE

Whole uncooked prawns are preferable in this recipe, but if using ready-cooked ones, simply warm them through in the delicious sauce.

◆

450 g/1 lb king prawns
30 ml/2 tbsp vegetable oil
3–4 dried red chillies, finely chopped
1 clove garlic, finely chopped
2.5 ml/½ tsp finely chopped ginger root
15 ml/1 tbsp light soy sauce
15 ml/1 tbsp Shao Hsing rice wine or dry sherry
5 ml/1 tsp chilli bean paste
5 ml/1 tsp tomato paste
15–30 ml/1–2 tbsp stock or water
2 spring onions, finely chopped
10 ml/2 tsp cornflour mixed with 15 ml/1 tbsp water
a few drops of sesame seed oil
lettuce leaves to garnish

◆

1 Preheat a browning dish according to the manufacturer's instructions – usually about 8 minutes.
2 Thaw the prawns, if necessary, then wash and dry on kitchen paper. Remove the heads, legs and tails, but keep the body shells on. Cut a slit along the back shell and carefully remove vein; cut into two or three pieces.
3 Sprinkle the oil in the hot browning dish, add the prawns and cook on HIGH for 2–3 minutes, or until they turn pink, turning once.
4 Add the chillies, garlic, ginger, soy sauce, wine, chilli bean paste, tomato paste and stock or water. Stir well and cook on HIGH for 1½ minutes, stirring constantly.
5 Add the spring onions and stir in the cornflour paste. Cook on MEDIUM for 30–40 seconds to thicken the sauce.
6 Sprinkle with the sesame seed oil and serve on a bed of lettuce leaves.

PRAWNS IN SWEET AND SOUR SAUCE

This recipe originated in Shanghai and you will find it quite different from the Cantonese version, with no gluey tomato ketchup or bits of pineapple.

◆

25 g/1 oz wood ears (black fungus)
225 g/8 oz uncooked prawns
5 ml/1 tsp salt
½ egg white, lightly beaten
10 ml/2 tsp cornflour mixed with 15 ml/1 tbsp water
about 6–8 water chestnuts
30 ml/2 tbsp vegetable oil
2.5 ml/½ tsp finely chopped ginger root
2 spring onions, finely chopped
15 ml/1 tbsp light soy sauce
15 ml/1 tbsp sugar
15 ml/1 tbsp vinegar
15 ml/1 tbsp Shao Hsing rice wine or dry sherry
15–30 ml/1–2 tbsp stock or water

◆

1 Soak the wood ears in warm water for 25–30 minutes.
2 Meanwhile, shell the prawns, remove the veins and dry thoroughly. Slice each prawn in half lengthways, but leave whole if small.
3 Sprinkle the prawns with a pinch of salt, mix with the egg white, and then the cornflour paste. Mix well.
4 Drain the water chestnuts and cut into slices.
5 Rinse the wood ears and discard any hard parts around the root.
6 Heat the oil on HIGH for about 1 minute; add the ginger and spring onions to flavour the oil for a few seconds.
7 Gently stir in the prawns and cook on HIGH for 1–1½ minutes, stirring twice.
8 Add the wood ears and water chestnuts, with the soy sauce, sugar, vinegar, wine and stock or water. Mix well and continue cooking on HIGH for 2–3 minutes, stirring.

Top: Fish Steak in Sweet and Sour Sauce; *bottom:* Chinese 'Paella'

CHINESE 'PAELLA'

As with the original Spanish dish, you can vary or substitute most of the ingredients in this recipe.

◆

225 g/8 oz long-grain rice
600 ml/1 pt boiling water
5 ml/1 tsp salt
225 g/8 oz pork or chicken, diced
225 g/8 oz squid, cleaned and cut into small rings
115 g/4 oz shellfish, such as scallops mussels or whelks
175 g/6 oz whole, uncooked prawns
1 carrot, diced
50 g/2 oz mushrooms, diced
1 red pepper, cored, seeded and diced
50 g/2 oz peas
1–2 spring onions, cut into short lengths
15 ml/1 tbsp vegetable oil
5 ml/1 tsp sugar
30 ml/2 tbsp light soy sauce
30 ml/2 tbsp Shao Hsing rice wine or dry sherry
15–30 ml/1–2 tbsp stock or water
5 ml/1 tsp sesame seed oil

◆

1 Wash the rice once in cold water, place in a large casserole, add the boiling water and cook on HIGH for 3–4 minutes under a vented lid.
2 Stir in half the salt, then add the meat and cook on HIGH for 2–3 minutes.
3 Add the remaining ingredients (except the sesame seed oil), mix well and cook on HIGH for 4–5 minutes, stirring once or twice. (If using cooked prawns, add them for the last minute of cooking time.)
4 Allow the dish to stand for 5 minutes, then sprinkle with the sesame seed oil and serve hot.

FISH STEAK IN SWEET AND SOUR SAUCE

For best results, use the small cutlets from the tail end of the fish.

◆

450 g/1 lb fish cutlets, such as cod, haddock or monkfish tails
1 egg, lightly beaten
30–45 ml/2–3 tbsp cornflour mixed with 30–45 ml/2–3 tbsp water
30–45 ml/2–3 tbsp vegetable oil
Sauce
25 ml/1½ tbsp sugar
15 ml/1 tbsp soy sauce
15 ml/1 tbsp Shao Hsing rice wine or dry sherry
15 ml/1 tbsp vinegar
1–2 spring onions, finely chopped
5 ml/1 tsp finely chopped ginger root
50 ml/2 fl oz stock or water
15 ml/1 tbsp cornflour mixed with 15 ml/1 tbsp water

◆

1 Preheat a browning dish according to the manufacturer's instructions – usually about 8 minutes.
2 Dry the fish well, otherwise they may fall apart during cooking.
3 Mix the beaten egg with the cornflour paste to make a light batter.
4 Heat the oil in the hot browning dish for 30–45 seconds. Dip the fish cutlets in the batter, coating both sides well. Arrange the cutlets on the browning dish, keeping them separate, and cook on HIGH for 2–3 minutes, or until they turn golden brown, turning two or three times.
5 Mix the sauce ingredients together and pour all over the fish; mix well and cook for 2–3 minutes on MEDIUM, stirring and shaking very gently three times. Serve hot.

FILLET OF SOLE WITH MUSHROOMS

This is my version of Filets de Sole Bonne Femme. *I am sure you will agree that my method is much simpler and – dare I say it? – perhaps even more delicious.*

◆

350–400 g/12–14 oz fillet of sole
1 egg white, lightly beaten
15 ml/1 tbsp cornflour mixed with 15 ml/1 tbsp cold water
115–175 g/4–6 oz fresh mushrooms
30–45 ml/2–3 tbsp vegetable oil
2 spring onions, cut into short lengths
1–2 slices ginger root, peeled and finely shredded
2.5 ml/½ tsp salt
2.5 ml/½ tsp sugar
15 ml/1 tbsp light soy sauce
15 ml/1 tbsp Shao Hsing rice wine or dry sherry
50 ml/2 fl oz stock
a few drops of sesame seed oil

◆

1 Pat dry the fillets and trim off the soft bones along the edges. Leave the fillets whole if small, otherwise cut in half.
2 Gently mix the fish with the egg white, then the cornflour.
3 Wash but do not peel the mushrooms, then slice thinly.
4 Heat the oil on HIGH for about 1 minute, then stir in the spring onions, ginger, mushrooms, salt, sugar, soy sauce, wine and stock; cook on HIGH for 1–2 minutes, stirring once or twice.
5 Add the fish to the sauce and braise on HIGH for 3–4 minutes, turning the fish very gently two or three times.
6 Sprinkle with the sesame seed oil and serve hot.

FISH FILLET IN WINE SAUCE PEKING-STYLE

Traditionally, fragrant fermented rice grains are used to flavour this dish, but they are not readily available in Britain. I find that the addition of a little brandy or whisky to rice wine or sherry produces almost the same effect.

◆

15 g/½ oz wood ears (black fungus)
450 g/1 lb filleted flat fish, such as plaice, sole or flounder
1 egg white, lightly beaten
30 ml/2 tbsp cornflour mixed with 45 ml/3 tbsp water
30 ml/2 tbsp vegetable oil
1–2 cloves garlic, crushed and finely chopped
5 ml/1 tsp salt
2.5 ml/½ tsp sugar
50 ml/2 fl oz stock
60 ml/4 tbsp Shao Hsing rice wine or dry sherry
15–30 ml/1–2 tbsp brandy or whisky
5 ml/1 tsp sesame seed oil

◆

1 Soak the wood ears in warm water for 25–30 minutes, then rinse clean and discard any hard bits.
2 Pat dry the fish, trim off the soft bones but leave the skin on. Cut into fairly large pieces and mix with the egg white, then half of the cornflour.
3 Heat the oil on HIGH for 1 minute, then add the garlic, wood ears, salt, sugar, stock, wine and brandy; mix well. Cook on HIGH for 1–2 minutes, or until boiling, stirring once or twice.
4 Add the fish piece by piece and mix gently to keep the pieces separate. Cook on HIGH for 3–4 minutes, turning the fish over very gently once or twice with chopsticks or tongs.
5 Add the remaining cornflour paste very slowly and evenly. Cook on MEDIUM for 30–40 seconds, or until the sauce thickens.
6 Sprinkle with the sesame seed oil and serve hot.

BRAISED MONKFISH TAILS

In China crabs are highly prized, particularly in the north since they are less abundant there than in the south. To compensate for the scarcity, recipes have been created to give certain types of fish a 'crab' flavour; this is one of them.

◆

450 g/1 lb monkfish tail fillets
15 ml/1 tbsp cornflour
4 egg whites, lightly beaten
30 ml/2 tbsp vegetable oil
30 ml/2 tbsp stock
5 ml/1 tsp salt
5 ml/1 tsp finely chopped spring onions
15 ml/1 tbsp Shao Hsing rice wine or dry sherry
10 ml/2 tsp vinegar
1–2 egg yolks (optional)
a few drops of sesame seed oil

◆

1 Skin and bone the fish, then cut into thin shreds. Coat with the cornflour then mix well with the egg whites.
2 Heat the oil on HIGH for about 1 minute. Stir in the fish shreds and cook on HIGH for 2–3 minutes, stirring very gently two or three times.
3 Stir in the stock, salt and ginger, then continue cooking for 1–2 minutes on HIGH, stirring gently once or twice.
4 Place the fish on a serving dish with the raw egg yolks on top, sprinkle with the sesame seed oil and bring the dish to the table. Break the yolks and stir into the fish just before serving.

RED-COOKED FISH

In China a fish weighing less than 900 g/2 lb is often cooked whole with head and tail intact. The fish is scored on both sides to allow the heat to penetrate more quickly and to help diffuse the flavour of the seasonings.

◆

550 g/1¼ lb fish, such as carp, sea bass, grey mullet or trout
30 ml/2 tbsp vegetable oil
2–3 slices ginger root, peeled and thinly shredded
2–3 spring onions, thinly shredded
15–30 ml/1–2 tbsp dark soy sauce
2.5 ml/½ tsp salt
2.5 ml/½ tsp sugar
15–30 ml/1–2 tbsp Shao Hsing rice wine or dry sherry
50 ml/2 fl oz stock or water
5 ml/1 tsp cornflour mixed with a little water
fresh coriander to garnish

◆

1 Scale, gut and clean the fish, if necessary. Dry thoroughly, then score both sides as deep as the bone with criss-cross diagonal cuts at intervals of about 2 cm/¾ in.
2 Heat the oil in a large shallow dish on HIGH for 30–40 seconds. Place about half the ginger and spring onions in the dish, position the fish on top and brush it with half the soy sauce. Place the remaining ginger and spring onions on top of the fish.
3 Cook on HIGH for 1 minute, then turn the fish over very gently, brush with the remaining soy sauce and cook on HIGH for 1 more minute.
4 Add the salt, sugar, wine and stock or water; cook on HIGH for 3–4 minutes, turning the fish over once or twice and basting it with the sauce now and again.
5 Lift fish carefully on to a serving plate.
6 Stir the cornflour paste into the sauce, cook on MEDIUM for 1 minute, or until smooth, then pour it over the fish. Garnish with fresh coriander. Serve hot or cold.

GREEN PEPPERS WITH PRAWN STUFFING

Prawn stuffing is also known as bark fa, *literally 'hundred flowers'.*

◆

175 g/6 oz peeled raw prawns
115 g/4 oz lean pork
50 g/2 oz pork fat
3–4 water chestnuts
2 spring onions, finely chopped
2.5 ml/½ tsp salt
15 ml/1 tbsp cornflour
3–4 small green peppers
30 ml/2 tbsp vegetable oil
15 ml/1 tbsp Shao Hsing rice wine or dry sherry
30 ml/2 tbsp light soy sauce
30–45 ml/2–3 tbsp stock or water

◆

1 Finely chop the prawns, pork, pork fat and water chestnuts, mix with about half the spring onions and the salt and cornflour. Blend or mix well to a smooth paste.

2 Cut the peppers in half lengthways, or quarter them if big, and discard the seeds; stuff the peppers with the prawn and pork mixture, and sprinkle a little cornflour over each.

3 Heat the oil in a preheated browning dish on HIGH, lay the stuffed peppers in the pan, meat side down, and cook on HIGH for 1–2 minutes, shaking and stirring gently once or twice.

4 Transfer the peppers to a shallow dish, meat side up, add the wine, soy sauce, stock or water and the remaining spring onions. Cover and cook on HIGH for 2–3 minutes, turning the peppers twice. Serve hot.

Left: Egg Fu-yung with Prawns or Crabmeat (page 60); *centre:* Lobster Cantonese in Black Bean Sauce (page 69); *right:* Green Peppers with Prawn Stuffing

BRAISED WHOLE FISH IN SWEET AND SOUR SAUCE

A slightly simplified version of the famous 'squirrel' fish from eastern China.

◆

3–4 dried Chinese mushrooms
550 g/1¼ lb fish, such as carp, bream, sea bass, grouper or grey mullet
5 ml/1 tsp salt
15 ml/1 tbsp Shao Hsing rice wine or dry sherry
30 ml/2 tbsp vegetable oil
50 g/2 oz bamboo shoots, diced
1 carrot, diced
25 g/1 oz peeled prawns
50 g/2 oz green peas
5 ml/1 tsp finely chopped ginger root
2 spring onions, finely chopped
15 ml/1 tbsp soy sauce
15 ml/1 tbsp sugar
15 ml/1 tbsp vinegar
15 ml/1 tbsp tomato paste
50 ml/2 fl oz stock or water
10 ml/2 tsp cornflour mixed with 15 ml/1 tbsp cold water

◆

1 Soak the mushrooms in warm water.
2 Meanwhile, scale, gut and clean the fish. Score both sides with several cuts as deep as the bone. Rub with salt both inside and out, and marinate in the wine for 10–15 minutes, turning once.
3 Squeeze the mushrooms dry, discard the hard stalks and cut into dice.
4 Preheat a browning dish according to the manufacturer's instructions – usually about 8 minutes. Sprinkle the oil into the hot dish and heat on HIGH for 40–45 seconds, then add the fish, curving it into the round dish if it is too long to lie flat; this will make an attractive shape. Cook on HIGH for 2 minutes, turning once.
5 Add the diced mushrooms, bamboo shoots, carrot, prawns, peas, ginger, spring onions, soy sauce, sugar, vinegar, tomato paste and stock or water, stir well and cook on HIGH for 2–3 minutes, or until boiling, stirring and turning frequently.
6 Stir in the cornflour paste and cook on MEDIUM for 1 minute, stirring to make it smooth. Serve immediately.

'CRYSTAL' PRAWNS

For best results, use whole uncooked prawns that are each about 5 cm/2 in long when the head is removed.

◆

675 g/1½ lb prawns
1 egg white, lightly beaten
15 ml/1 tbsp cornflour mixed with 15 ml/1 tbsp cold water
15–30 ml/1–2 tbsp vegetable oil
5 ml/1 tsp finely chopped ginger root
2 spring onions (white parts only), finely chopped
5 ml/1 tsp salt
15 ml/1 tbsp Shao Hsing rice wine or dry sherry
30 ml/2 tbsp stock

◆

1 Thaw the prawns, if necessary, then remove the heads, shells and veins; wash under cold running water for at least 10 minutes, or until the water is clean. Dry thoroughly on kitchen paper.
2 Stir the prawns into the egg white, then into the cornflour paste; blend well, then cover and refrigerate for 3 hours.
3 Heat the oil on HIGH for about 1 minute; add the ginger and spring onions, cook on HIGH for about 30–40 seconds.
4 Mix in the prawns and cook on MEDIUM for 3–4 minutes, stirring frequently.
5 Add the salt, wine and stock; cook for 1 minute more, stirring once or twice. *Do not overcook.* The prawns should look bright white like crystal, and taste so delicious and tender that they almost melt in your mouth. Serve hot.

BRAISED FISH IN HOT BEAN SAUCE

This is the Sichuan version of red-cooked fish. The method is almost the same, but the result has a distinctively different flavour.

◆

675 g/1½ lb fish, such as carp, sea bass, trout or grey mullet
2–3 spring onions
30 ml/2 tbsp vegetable oil
1–2 cloves garlic, finely chopped
5 ml/1 tsp finely chopped ginger root
15 ml/1 tbsp chilli bean paste
15 ml/1 tbsp tomato paste
15 ml/1 tbsp soy sauce
2.5 ml/½ tsp salt
5 ml/1 tsp sugar
30 ml/2 tbsp Shao Hsing rice wine or dry sherry
150 ml/5 fl oz stock or water
15 ml/1 tbsp vinegar
15 ml/1 tbsp cornflour mixed with a little water

◆

1 Scale, gut and clean the fish, discarding the head and tail. Dry well, then slash both sides diagonally as deep as the bone at intervals of about 2 cm/¾ in.

2 Finely chop the spring onions, keeping the white and green parts separate.

3 Heat the oil in a large shallow dish on HIGH for 40–50 seconds; add the garlic, ginger and white parts of the spring onions to flavour the oil for about 30 seconds, then add the fish. Cook on HIGH for 2 minutes, turning once.

4 Add the chilli bean paste, tomato paste, soy sauce, salt, sugar, wine and stock or water. Cook on HIGH for 3–4 minutes, or until boiling, turning the fish twice.

5 Carefully lift the fish on to a plate.

6 Add the vinegar and green parts of the spring onions to the sauce, then stir in the cornflour paste; cook on HIGH for 1 minute, stirring until smooth, then pour it over the fish and serve immediately.

LOBSTER CANTONESE IN BLACK BEAN SAUCE

Try to use live lobsters, if you can, as ready-cooked lobsters tend to lack flavour.

◆

1 large or 2 medium lobsters, weighing about 675 g/1½ lb in total
30 ml/2 tbsp Shao Hsing rice wine or dry sherry
15 ml/1 tbsp soy sauce
15 ml/1 tbsp cornflour
30–45 ml/2–3 tbsp vegetable oil
1 clove garlic, finely chopped
5–10 ml/1–2 tsp finely chopped ginger root
2–3 spring onions, finely chopped
30 ml/2 tbsp salted black beans crushed with
15 ml/1 tbsp rice wine
15 ml/1 tbsp vinegar
50 ml/2 fl oz stock or water

◆

1 Provided you possess nerve and a very sharp knife (a Chinese cleaver is ideal), the best way of killing a live lobster is to cut lengthways through its head, then work your way down the body to the tail, so that you end up with two halves. Carefully remove the two claws and crack them with the back of a cleaver. Discard the feathery lungs and intestine, but reserve the dark green juices in the head – they turn bright orange when cooked and are most delicious. Cut each lobster half into 4.

2 Mix together the wine, soy sauce and cornflour, and marinate the lobster pieces for 10–15 minutes.

3 Heat the oil in a casserole on HIGH for 40–50 seconds, add the garlic, ginger, spring onions and crushed black beans, mix well and cook on HIGH for 1 minute.

4 Add the lobster pieces, stir well and cook on HIGH for 2–3 minutes, or until the lobster has turned bright orange, stirring.

5 Add the vinegar and stock or water. Continue cooking on HIGH for 2–3 minutes more, until boiling, stirring.

CRAB WITH SPRING ONIONS AND GINGER

As this Cantonese dish is best eaten with your fingers, have finger bowls of warm water with a segment or two of lemon on the table, plus lots of paper tissues. Lobster also lends itself to this recipe.

◆

1 large or 2 medium crabs, weighing about
675 g/1½ lb in total
30 ml/2 tbsp Shao Hsing rice wine or dry sherry
1 egg, lightly beaten
15 ml/1 tbsp cornflour
30–45 ml/2–3 tbsp vegetable oil
1 clove garlic, crushed
15 ml/1 tbsp finely chopped ginger root
3–4 spring onions, finely chopped
30 ml/2 tbsp light soy sauce
5 ml/1 tsp sugar
50 ml/2 fl oz stock or water

◆

1 Break the legs and claws off the crabs and crack them with the back of a Chinese cleaver or heavy knife; crack the shell and break it into several pieces; discard the feathery gills and the sac.

2 Mix together the wine, egg and cornflour, stir in the crab pieces and leave to marinate for 10–15 minutes.

3 Preheat a browning dish according to the manufacturer's instructions – usually about 8 minutes. Add the oil and garlic, heat on HIGH 40–50 seconds, then discard the garlic.

4 Cook the crab pieces in batches on HIGH for 1–2 minutes, stirring once or twice.

5 Transfer the partly-cooked pieces to a casserole, add the ginger, spring onions, soy sauce and sugar, mix well and add the stock or water; cook on HIGH for 3–4 minutes, stirring frequently. Serve immediately.

Left: Crab with Spring Onions and Ginger; *centre:* Braised Whole Fish in Sweet and Sour Sauce (page 68); *right:* Perfect Rice (page 112)

STEAMED WHOLE FISH WITH 'WHITE' SAUCE

This recipe comes from Hubei in central China, known as 'the province of a thousand lakes' as well as 'land of fish and rice', so it's no surprise that fish cookery is one of the region's specialities.

◆

550–575 g/1¼–1½ lb fish, such as perch, bream, carp, trout, sea bass or sole
2–3 dried Chinese mushrooms
salt
30 ml/2 tbsp Shao Hsing rice wine or dry sherry
25 g/1 oz bamboo shoots
25 g/1 oz cooked ham
2–3 spring onions
2–3 slices ginger root, peeled
30 ml/2 tbsp oil
1–2 spring onions, finely chopped
5 ml/1 tsp finely chopped ginger root
25 g/1 oz peeled prawns
25 g/1 oz peas
50 ml/2 fl oz stock
5 ml/1 tsp cornflour mixed with 15 ml/1 tbsp milk

◆

1 Soak mushrooms for 20–25 minutes.
2 Scale, gut and clean the fish. Score both sides of the fish as deep as the bone at intervals of about 2 cm/¾ in. Rub the salt inside and out then marinate in the wine for 3–5 minutes.
3 Squeeze the mushrooms dry, discard the hard stalks and cut into dice.
4 Dice the bamboo shoots and ham.
5 Arrange 1 or 2 whole spring onions and half the sliced ginger on the ribbed rack of an all-purpose cooker, insert the fish and put the remaining spring onion and ginger on top. Fill the base pan with boiling water and steam on HIGH for 3–4 minutes per 450 g/1 lb. Lift on to a serving dish.
6 Heat the oil on HIGH for 40–50 seconds, add the spring onion, ginger, prawns, peas, mushrooms, ham and bamboo shoots, stir well and cook on HIGH for about 1 minute.
7 Add salt and stock and continue cooking on HIGH for about 1 minute.
8 Stir in the cornflour paste and cook on MEDIUM for 40–50 seconds, stirring frequently. Pour over fish.

FISH AND BEAN CURD IN HOT AND SOUR SAUCE

This dish comes from my mother's province, Jiangxi, in south-east China.

◆

450 g/1 lb fish fillet, such as cod, sole or haddock
30 ml/2 tbsp light soy sauce
30 ml/2 tbsp vegetable oil
2 spring onions, finely chopped
1 clove garlic, crushed and finely chopped
5 ml/1 tsp finely chopped ginger root
2 cakes bean curd, diced
2.5 ml/½ tsp salt
30 ml/2 tbsp Shao Hsing rice wine or dry sherry
2.5 ml/½ tsp sugar
15 ml/1 tbsp chilli bean paste
15 ml/1 tbsp vinegar
15–30 ml/1–2 tbsp stock or water
fresh coriander leaves to garnish

◆

1 Cut the fish into 5 cm/2 in pieces, sprinkle with about 15 ml/1 tbsp soy sauce and leave to marinate for about 5 minutes.
2 Heat the oil in a preheated browning dish, place the fish slices in a single layer and cook on HIGH for 2 minutes, gently turning once.
3 Transfer the fish to a casserole, add all the remaining ingredients (except the coriander), and mix well. Cover and cook on HIGH for 3–4 minutes, or until boiling, stirring and shaking very gently twice.
4 Garnish with coriander leaves.

STEAMED FISH IN BLACK BEAN SAUCE CANTON-STYLE

For best results, use an all-purpose cooker, placing the fish on the ribbed rack above boiling water in the base pan. When covered, the fish cooks gently in the steam.

◆

675g/1½lb fish, such as sea bass, trout, grey mullet, sole or turbot
2.5 ml/½ tsp salt
5 ml/1 tsp sesame seed oil
2–3 spring onions
15 ml/1 tbsp salted black beans
15 ml/1 tbsp light soy sauce
30 ml/2 tbsp Shao Hsing rice wine or dry sherry
2–3 slices ginger root, peeled and thinly shredded
15–30 ml/1–2 tbsp oil
2 spring onions, finely shredded

◆

1 Scale, clean and dry the fish thoroughly, then score on both sides as deep as the bone at intervals of about 2 cm/¾ in. Rub inside the fish with salt and sesame seed oil (this is not necessary for flat fish). Place the whole spring onions on the ribbed steamer rack and sit the fish on top. If it is too long to fit the rack, lightly tie the head and tail into a gentle curve with string.
2 Fill the base of the pan with boiling water, place the rack on top, cover and cook on HIGH for 3–4 minutes per 450 g/1 lb for a round fish, or 3 minutes for a flat fish, turning once. When done, lift the fish gently on to a serving dish, discarding the spring onions and string.
3 Crush the black beans and mix in a jug with the soy sauce, wine, ginger, and oil. Heat on HIGH for 2 minutes, stirring once or twice.
4 Pour the sauce over the whole length of the fish and arrange the shredded spring onions on top. Serve hot.

CANTONESE STUFFED BEAN CURD IN OYSTER SAUCE

A variation of the prawn stuffing from the Hakka school. Although this dish may appear complicated, it is well worth the effort.

◆

2 dried Chinese mushrooms
6 cakes bean curd
115 g/4 oz pork (not too lean)
50 g/2 oz fish fillet
50 g/2 oz peeled raw prawns
2 spring onions, finely chopped
2.5 ml/½ tsp salt
15 ml/1 tbsp Shao Hsing rice wine or dry sherry
15 ml/1 tbsp light soy sauce
10 ml/2 tsp cornflour
30–45 ml/2–3 tbsp vegetable oil
30 ml/2 tbsp oyster sauce
15–30 ml/1–2 tbsp stock or water

◆

1 Soak the mushrooms in warm water for 20–25 minutes.
2 Harden the bean curd by blanching it in a pan of lightly-salted boiling water for 2–3 minutes. Remove and drain; cut each cake into 4 triangular pieces.
3 Squeeze the mushrooms dry and discard the stalks.
4 Coarsely chop the pork, fish, prawns and mushrooms. Mix with about half the spring onions plus the salt, wine, soy sauce and cornflour; stir well.
5 Cut a slit on one side of each bean curd triangle and stuff with the mixture.
6 Heat the oil in a preheated browning dish, arrange the stuffed bean curd in single layer and cook on HIGH for 2–3 minutes, turning once.
7 Transfer the bean curd to a shallow dish, add the oyster sauce and a little stock or water, cover and cook on HIGH for 2–3 minutes, stirring very gently once or twice. Garnish with spring onions.

POULTRY

IN CHINA CHICKEN IS REGARDED *as especially nutritious and is often treated as a greater delicacy than pork. It is eaten at both festivals and everyday meals, but duck is only prepared on special occasions at home. There are a number of reasons for this, one of them being that chickens are reared in virtually every household, while ducks are not; they are more often produced in large flocks on lakes, ponds and waterways.*

Chicken is very versatile as it can be cooked in so many different ways, combined with almost any other ingredient, and yet still retain its characteristic texture and flavour. By comparison, a duck produces little meat and has a great deal of fat, skin and bones. This means that it is best suited to roasting, which drains off excess fat, retains the tenderness of the meat and, above all, renders the skin crispy and delicious. Since most Chinese homes have simple stoves but no ovens, a Chinese family would expect to eat roast duck only in restaurants or buy it from take-aways.

As you will have gathered, almost all Chinese poultry is free-range; the meat may be a little tough, but is full of natural flavour. You have no doubt noticed the difference between free-range and battery-reared chickens: one is juicily succulent, the other dry and tasteless. There is even a noticeable difference between the cellophane-wrapped bird that has been chilled for days in the supermarket and the fresh-killed poultry in a traditional family butcher.

Nowadays, portions of chicken, such as breasts, wings, thighs and drumsticks, can all be bought separately, but it is more economical to buy a whole chicken from your favourite supplier and to joint it yourself. This ensures the quality and freshness of the meat, and you can use the discarded bits and pieces for stock-making.

SHREDDED CHICKEN WITH CELERY

One of my personal favourites, this simple dish contrasts tender chicken with the crunchy texture of celery. I learnt the original recipe from the Sichuan chef Tsao-Bing, formerly of the Dragon Gate Restaurant, now co-proprietor of the Si Chuen Restaurant in London.

◆

2 chicken breasts, boned and skinned
5 ml/1 tsp salt
½ egg white, lightly beaten
10 ml/2 tsp cornflour mixed with a little water
1 celery heart or 3–4 stalks tender celery
1–2 red or green hot chillies, seeded
30 ml/2 tbsp vegetable oil
2 spring onions, thinly shredded
2 slices ginger root, peeled and thinly shredded
2.5 ml/½ tsp sugar
10 ml/2 tsp light soy sauce
15 ml/1 tbsp Shao Hsing rice wine or dry sherry

◆

1 Remove the white tendon and membrane from the chicken, then thinly shred the meat into matchstick slivers. Mix first with a pinch of salt, then the egg white, and finally the cornflour paste; mix well with your fingers.
2 Thinly shred the celery and chillies to the same size as the chicken.
3 Heat the oil on HIGH for 40–50 seconds, add the chicken shreds and stir gently with chopsticks to separate. Cook on MEDIUM for 1–2 minutes, or until the meat becomes white, stirring once or twice during cooking.
4 Add the chillies, spring onions, ginger, celery, salt, sugar, soy sauce and wine, stir well and cook on HIGH for 2–3 minutes, stirring frequently. Serve hot or cold.

CHICKEN FU-YUNG

Fu-yung *means creamy-textured egg whites. When cooked in the conventional way, it is briefly deep-fried, which has prompted certain imaginative cooks to call this dish 'deep-fried milk'!*

◆

115 g/4 oz filleted chicken breast meat
15 ml/1 tbsp cornflour mixed with 30 ml/2 tbsp milk
5–6 egg whites, lightly beaten
2.5 ml/½ tsp salt
30 ml/2 tbsp vegetable oil
50 ml/2 fl oz chicken stock
15 ml/1 tbsp Shao Hsing rice wine or dry sherry
25 g/1 oz peas
25 g/1 oz cooked ham, finely chopped
a few drops of sesame seed oil

◆

1 Ideally, use the two tenderest strips of chicken meat just along the breastbone. Pound the meat with the blunt edge of a cleaver for about 5 minutes, adding a little cold water now and again. Then chop the meat with the sharp edge of the blade for a further 5–10 minutes, or until the meat has a creamy texture.
2 Make a smooth paste with the cornflour and milk; add the chicken meat, egg whites and a pinch of salt. Mix well.
3 Heat the oil on HIGH for 40–50 seconds, stir in the chicken mixture and cook on MEDIUM for 2–3 minutes, or until just set, stirring frequently.
4 Add the stock, salt, wine and peas, stir and cook on HIGH for 1–2 minutes, stirring once or twice.
5 Sprinkle the fu-yung with the ham and sesame seed oil. Serve hot and eat with spoon.

RED-COOKED CHICKEN

Probably the most popular method of cooking chicken in China. The main feature of this dish is a plentiful rich sauce, to which one can add vegetables, such as bamboo shoots, mushrooms or carrots, to absorb the savouriness and harmonize the flavours.

1 young chicken weighing about 1.5 kg/3–3½ lb
3 slices ginger root, peeled
2–3 spring onions
5 ml/1 tsp salt
15 ml/1 tbsp sugar
30–45 ml/2–3 tbsp Shao Hsing rice wine or dry sherry
45 ml/3 tbsp dark soy sauce
300 ml/½ pt stock or water

1 Joint the chicken, then chop it through the bone into 20–24 bite-size pieces.

2 Chop the ginger root into small pieces, and the spring onions into short lengths.

3 Brown the chicken pieces in a preheated browning dish on HIGH for 2–3 minutes, stirring once or twice.

4 Transfer the chicken to a casserole, add all the remaining ingredients, mix well and cook under a vented lid on HIGH for 3–4 minutes, or until boiling, stirring once or twice. If you wish, you can add 225–275 g/8–10 oz diced vegetables at this stage.

5 Continue cooking on MEDIUM for 3–4 minutes, stirring once or twice. Leave the chicken to stand for 10 minutes before serving.

BRAISED CHICKEN IN BROWN SAUCE

Chicken legs (including both thighs and drumsticks) are ideal for this dish.

4 chicken legs (or 4 thighs and 4 drumsticks)
2.5 ml/½ tsp salt
15 ml/1 tbsp sugar
15 ml/1 tbsp dark soy sauce
30 ml/2 tbsp Shao Hsing rice wine or dry sherry
10 ml/2 tsp cornflour
15 ml/1 tbsp vegetable oil
2 cloves garlic, crushed
2–3 spring onions, cut into short lengths
2 dried red chillies, seeded and chopped
30 ml/2 tbsp crushed yellow bean paste
120 ml/4 fl oz stock or water

1 Chop each thigh and drumstick through the bone into 3 or 4 bite-size pieces.

2 Mix the chicken with the salt, sugar, soy sauce and wine, add the cornflour and oil and marinate for 15–20 minutes, stirring once or twice.

3 Brown the chicken pieces in a preheated browning dish on HIGH for 1–2 minutes, stirring once or twice.

4 Transfer the chicken to a casserole, add the garlic, the white parts of the spring onions, chillies, bean paste and stock or water, and mix well. Cover with a vented lid and cook on HIGH for 4–5 minutes, or until boiling, stirring once or twice.

5 Add the green parts of the spring onions and cook on MEDIUM for 2–3 minutes more, stirring once. Serve hot.

Bottom left: Sichuan 'Kung-po' Chicken with Cashew Nuts (page 80); *top centre:* Chicken and Mushrooms; *right:* Chicken Slices and Vegetables (page 80)

CHICKEN AND MUSHROOMS

Simplicity itself to make, yet delicious, colourful and nutritious.

◆

2 chicken breasts, boned and skinned
2.5 ml/½ tsp salt
½ egg white, lightly beaten
10 ml/2 tsp cornflour mixed with a little water
30 ml/2 tbsp vegetable oil
225 g/8 oz white mushrooms
6–8 water chestnuts
115 g/4 oz peas
2 spring onions, cut into short lengths
2.5 ml/½ tsp sugar
15 ml/1 tbsp light soy sauce
15 ml/1 tbsp Shao Hsing rice wine or dry sherry
a few drops of sesame seed oil (optional)

◆

1 Remove the white tendon and membrane from the chicken and cut the meat into thin slices about the size of an oblong postage stamp.
2 Sprinkle the meat with half the salt, then stir in the egg white, the cornflour paste and, finally, about 5 ml/1 tsp oil. Mix well.
3 Thinly slice the mushrooms and water chestnuts.
4 Cook the chicken on MEDIUM for 2–3 minutes, or until it turns white, stirring once or twice.
5 Add all the remaining ingredients, except the sesame seed oil, mix well and cook on HIGH for 2–3 minutes, stirring once.
6 Add the sesame seed oil (if using) and serve the dish hot.

CHICKEN SLICES AND VEGETABLES

◆

4–5 dried Chinese mushrooms
225–275 g/8–10 oz chicken meat, boned and skinned
15 ml/1 tbsp Shao Hsing rice wine or dry sherry
5 ml/1 tsp salt
½ egg white, lightly beaten
15 ml/1 tbsp cornflour mixed with 15 ml/1 tbsp water
115 g/4 oz bamboo shoots
115 g/4 oz green vegetable, such as spinach or mange-tout
30 ml/2 tbsp vegetable oil
2 spring onions, cut into short lengths
1 slice ginger root, peeled and chopped
2.5 ml/½ tsp sugar
15 ml/1 tbsp light soy sauce
5 ml/1 tsp sesame seed oil

◆

1 Soak mushrooms for 20–25 minutes.
2 Cut the chicken meat into thin slices about the size of a postage stamp; mix first with the wine, then a pinch of salt, the egg white and about half the cornflour paste.
3 Squeeze the mushrooms dry and discard the hard stalks.
4 Cut the mushrooms, bamboo shoots and green vegetable into small pieces.
5 Heat the oil on HIGH for 40–50 seconds, add the chicken, stir and cook on MEDIUM for 1–2 minutes, or until the meat turns white. (If using pork or lamb for this dish, cook on MEDIUM for 3–4 minutes; cook beef, liver or kidney on HIGH for 1–2 minutes, stirring once or twice.)
6 Add the spring onions, ginger, vegetables, salt, sugar and soy sauce, stir well and cook on HIGH for 2–3 minutes, stirring frequently.
7 Add the remaining cornflour paste to thicken the liquid. Continue cooking on MEDIUM for 30–40 seconds, stirring once or twice. Serve hot sprinkled with sesame seed oil.

SICHUAN 'KUNG-PO' CHICKEN WITH CASHEW NUTS

This is a very popular dish named after a court official from Sichuan. The cashews can be substituted with walnuts, peanuts or almonds.

◆

275–350 g/10–12 oz chicken meat, boned and skinned
2.5 ml/½ tsp salt
1 egg white, lightly beaten
15 ml/1 tbsp cornflour mixed with 15 ml/1 tbsp cold water
1 green pepper, cored and seeded
50 g/2 oz cashew nuts, shelled
30 ml/2 tbsp vegetable oil
2 spring onions, cut into short lengths
1–2 slices ginger root, peeled and chopped
3–4 dried red chillies
2.5 ml/½ tsp sugar
15 ml/1 tbsp Sichuan chilli bean paste
30 ml/2 tbsp Shao Hsing rice wine or dry sherry

◆

1 Cut the chicken meat into small cubes about the size of sugar lumps. Mix first with the salt, then the egg white and finally about half the cornflour paste. Mix well with your fingers.
2 Cut the green peppers into pieces the same size as the chicken cubes. Split the cashew nuts into half.
3 Heat the oil on HIGH for 40–50 seconds, add the chicken cubes, stir and cook on MEDIUM for 1–2 minutes, or until the meat turns white, stirring once or twice.
4 Add the spring onions, ginger, chillies, green peppers, cashew nuts, sugar, bean paste and wine, mix well and cook on HIGH for 2–3 minutes, stirring frequently.
5 Thicken the liquid with the remaining cornflour paste, mix well and cook on MEDIUM for 30–40 seconds, stirring once or twice. Serve hot.

DRUNKEN CHICKEN

This dish is also known as 'Imperial Concubine Chicken', in memory of the Empress Yang Kwei-fei of the Tang dynasty, a concubine noted for her fondness of alcohol as well as her beauty.

◆

1.25 kg/2½–2¾ lb young chicken
150 ml/¼ pt Shao Hsing rice wine or dry sherry
25 ml/1 fl oz brandy
10 ml/2 tsp salt
5 ml/1 tsp Sichuan peppercorns
2 slices ginger root, peeled
2 spring onions, cut into short lengths
fresh coriander leaves to garnish

◆

1 Clean and dry the chicken well, place it in a casserole, cover with boiling water and cook on HIGH for 2 minutes. Drain and rinse with cold water.
2 Add the wine and brandy to the casserole, stir in the salt, peppercorns, ginger and spring onions. Return the chicken to the casserole, breast-side down, cover with a vented lid and cook on HIGH for 20–25 minutes, turning over halfway through cooking.
3 Place the chicken breast-side up on a serving dish, cover loosely with foil and leave to stand for 10 minutes.
4 Serve the chicken whole or chopped into bite-size pieces (see p.8). (The chicken should be so tender that you can take it to pieces with a pair of chopsticks.)
5 Season the cooking liquid to taste, reheat if necessary and pour over the chicken; garnish with coriander leaves.

HUNAN CHICKEN IN SPICY SAUCE

Also known as 'Dong An Chicken', after the small town in Hunan from which this very popular dish originated.

◆

3–4 dried Chinese mushrooms
900 g/2 lb young chicken
3–4 dried red chillies
2 slices ginger root, peeled
2 spring onions
5 ml/1 tsp crushed Sichuan peppercorns
15 ml/1 tbsp vegetable oil
5 ml/1 tsp salt
15 ml/1 tbsp soy sauce
15 ml/1 tbsp vinegar
30 ml/2 tbsp Shao Hsing rice wine or brandy
50 ml/2 fl oz stock or water
10 ml/2 tsp cornflour mixed with 15 ml/1 tbsp water
5 ml/1 tsp sesame seed oil

◆

1 Soak the mushrooms in warm water for 20–25 minutes.
2 Place the chicken in a casserole, cover with boiling water and cook on HIGH for 3–4 minutes; remove and rinse in cold water. When it has cooled a little, take the meat off the bone (keeping the skin on), and cut into long, thin strips.
3 Squeeze the mushrooms dry, discarding any hard parts.
4 Thinly shred the mushrooms, ginger and spring onions.
5 Heat the oil in a casserole with the chillies, ginger, spring onions and peppercorns for about 1 minute, then add the chicken, mushrooms, salt, soy sauce, vinegar, wine and 3–4 tbsp of the cooking liquid; mix well and cook on HIGH for 3–4 minutes, stirring once or twice.
6 Add the cornflour paste, mix well and cook on MEDIUM for 40–50 seconds.
7 Add the sesame seed oil and serve hot.

ROAST CHICKEN CANTON-STYLE

You have probably seen this bright brown chicken hanging in the windows of some Cantonese restaurants. The skin is coated with soy sauce, honey and sesame seed oil, which gives the bird a lacquered appearance.

◆

1.5 kg/3–3½ lb roasting chicken
5 ml/1 tsp salt
15 ml/1 tbsp oil
5 ml/1 tsp finely chopped ginger root
2 spring onions, finely chopped
15 ml/1 tbsp sugar
15 ml/1 tbsp Hoi Sin sauce
30 ml/2 tbsp Shao Hsing rice wine or dry sherry
10 ml/2 tsp five-spice powder
30 ml/2 tbsp honey dissolved in 50 ml/2 fl oz hot water
30–45 ml/2–3 tbsp dark soy sauce
15 ml/1 tbsp sesame seed oil

◆

1 Clean the chicken well and pat dry with cloth or paper inside and out. Rub both inside and out with salt.
2 Heat the oil in a small jug on HIGH for 30–40 seconds, add the ginger root, spring onions, sugar, Hoi Sin sauce, wine and five-spice powder, mix well and bring to the boil (about 1–2 minutes), stirring once or twice. Pour the liquid into the cavity of the chicken, and sew it up securely.
3 Plunge the whole chicken into a large pot of boiling water for a few seconds only; take it out and brush it thoroughly with half the honey, then with half the soy sauce, and hang it up to dry for at least 2–3 hours.
4 Weigh the chicken and calculate the cooking time based on 7–8 minutes per 450 g/1 lb.
5 Place the chicken breast-side down on a roasting rack, place the rack inside a large roasting bag and fold the open end lightly underneath. Cook on HIGH.

6 Half way through cooking, remove the chicken and rack from the roasting bag and pour off any fat. Replace the chicken on the rack, breast-side uppermost, brush with the remaining honey and soy sauce and complete the cooking uncovered.
7 When done, remove the chicken from the oven, brush with sesame seed oil, then cover with foil. Stand 10–15 minutes.
8 To serve, remove the strings and pour the liquid into a bowl or jug; chop the chicken into small, bite-size pieces, pour the cooking liquid over it and serve.

STEAMED CHICKEN WITH CHINESE MUSHROOMS

◆

3–4 dried Chinese mushrooms
675 g/1½ lb chicken breasts and/or thighs
15 ml/1 tbsp light soy sauce
15 ml/1 tbsp Shao Hsing rice wine or dry sherry
5 ml/1 tsp sugar
10 ml/2 tsp cornflour
2 slices ginger root, peeled and thinly shredded
5 ml/1 tsp sesame seed oil
salt and pepper to taste

◆

1 Soak the mushrooms in warm water.
2 Chop the chicken through the bone into bite-size pieces.
3 Mix together the soy sauce, wine, sugar and cornflour, add the chicken and marinate for 25–30 minutes.
4 Squeeze the mushrooms dry, discarding the hard stalks; shred thinly.
5 Place the chicken pieces in a shallow casserole and top with the mushrooms and ginger. Cover with a vented lid and cook on HIGH for 8–10 minutes, stirring once.
6 Sprinkle with the sesame seed oil, adjust the seasoning and serve hot.

Top: Noodles (page 110); *centre:* Roast Chicken Canton-style; *bottom:* Diced Chicken with Green Peppers (page 84)

DICED CHICKEN WITH GREEN PEPPERS

I learned this dish from my mother, who originally learned it from her mother in Jiangxi, south-east China. For extra colour, use one red and one green pepper.

◆

2 chicken breasts, boned and skinned
5 ml/1 tsp salt
½ egg white, lightly beaten
10 ml/2 tsp cornflour mixed with 15 ml/1 tbsp water
1–2 green peppers, cored and seeded
30 ml/2 tbsp vegetable oil
2 spring onions, cut into short lengths
2.5 ml/½ tsp sugar
15 ml/1 tbsp Shao Hsing rice wine or dry sherry
a few drops of sesame seed oil

◆

1 Remove the white tendon and membrane from the chicken breasts. Cut the meat into small cubes the size of sugar lumps, then mix with a pinch of salt, the egg white, and finally the cornflour paste. Mix well with your fingers.
2 Cut the peppers to the same size as the chicken cubes.
3 Heat the oil on HIGH for 40–50 seconds, add the chicken cubes, stir and cook on HIGH for 1–2 minutes, stirring once or twice.
4 Add the spring onions, peppers, salt, sugar and wine. Stir and cook on HIGH for 2–3 minutes, stirring frequently.
5 Sprinkle with the sesame seed oil and serve immediately.

CHICKEN CUBES WITH CUCUMBER

The cucumber is peeled in the orthodox version of this recipe from Canton, but I always leave the skin on to give the dish extra colour and flavour.

◆

2 chicken breasts, boned and skinned
5 ml/1 tsp salt
½ egg white, lightly beaten
10 ml/2 tsp cornflour mixed with a little cold water
1 medium cucumber
30 ml/2 tbsp vegetable oil
1–2 cloves garlic, crushed
2 spring onions, cut into short lengths
15 ml/1 tbsp Shao Hsing rice wine or dry sherry
15 ml/1 tbsp light soy sauce
a few drops of sesame seed oil

◆

1 Remove the white tendon and membrane from the chicken breasts and dice the meat into small cubes; mix in a pinch of salt, then the egg white, and finally the cornflour paste.
2 Cut the cucumber into roughly the same shape and size as the chicken cubes.
3 Heat the oil on HIGH for 40–50 seconds, add the chicken cubes, stir and cook on MEDIUM for 2–3 minutes, or until the meat turns white, stirring once or twice.
4 Add the garlic, spring onions and cucumber, stir and cook on HIGH for 2–3 minutes, stirring once or twice; add the salt, wine and soy sauce during the last 30 seconds or so.
5 Add the sesame seed oil, mix together well and serve hot.

ROAST DUCK PEKING-STYLE

The original recipe for this dish, using a specially reared duck, runs into several thousand words, starting with a detailed description of how to make up the duck feed and continuing with complicated instructions on how to build and fire the oven. Here is a simplified version using a fresh (definitely not frozen) Aylesbury duck. The most important point to remember is that the skin of the duck must be absolutely dry before cooking. The pancakes required in this dish can be bought ready-made from most Chinese Supermarkets. If you have difficulty finding them, use Greek pitta bread instead. Hoi Sin sauce may also be substituted for the homemade sauce in this recipe.

◆

2.25 kg/5–5¼ lb oven-ready duckling
30 ml/2 tbsp honey dissolved in 300 ml/½ pt warm water and 15 ml/1 tbsp vinegar
dark soy sauce
24 thin pancakes (see p.113)
1 medium cucumber
1 bunch spring onions
Sauce
15 ml/1 tbsp sesame seed oil
120 ml/8 tbsp crushed yellow bean paste
30 ml/2 tbsp sugar

◆

1 Clean the duck well and cut off the wings. Plunge the bird into a pot of boiling water for 2–3 minutes in order to seal the pores; this will make the skin airtight, preventing the fat from escaping while it is being roasted.

2 Brush the duck all over with the honey and vinegar solution while the skin is still hot, then hang it up to dry in a cool, well ventilated spot for at least 4 hours. (Use a fan heater or a hairdryer if you want to speed up the process.)

3 Weigh the duck and calculate the cooking time based on 7–10 minutes per 450 g/ 1 lb. Place the duck breast-side down on a roasting rack and brush with soy sauce; put the duck and rack in a large roasting bag and lightly tuck the open end underneath.

4 Cook the bird on HIGH for half the cooking time, then remove and pour off any fat. Replace the duck on the rack, breast-side uppermost, and brush with soy sauce. Complete the cooking uncovered.

5 Remove the duck, cover lightly with foil and leave to stand for 10–12 minutes.

6 Arrange the pancakes, overlapping, in a roasting bag. Fold the open end underneath and cook on HIGH for 2–2 ½ minutes if frozen, 1½-2 minutes if fresh; they should be soft and hot. Remove from the roasting bag and wrap in a napkin to keep warm.

7 Cut the cucumber into thin strips the size of matchsticks; thinly shred the spring onions.

8 Mix the sauce ingredients together in a small bowl and cook on HIGH for 45–55 seconds, or until smooth and bubbling.

9 Just before serving, cut the duck in half along the back and breastbone and place on a grill rack skin-side uppermost. Cook under a preheated grill until the skin is crisp and a rich, dark brown.

10 Peel off the crispy skin in small slices using a sharp carving knife and place on a small serving plate. Carve the meat and arrange on a separate dish.

11 Spread 2.5 ml/½ tsp of the sauce over a pancake, place a few strips of cucumber and spring onions in the centre, add 1 or 2 slices of crispy skin and 2 or 3 slices of duck meat, then roll up the pancake, tucking in the ends to prevent the sauce from oozing out. Eat with your fingers like a sausage roll.

Note The duck carcass is traditionally made into a delicious soup and served with Chinese leaves and with seasonings at the end of the meal (see p.14).

Top: Eight-treasure Duck; *bottom:* Chicken Cubes with Cucumber (page 84)

EIGHT-TREASURE DUCK

◆

2kg/4½–4¾lb duckling, with giblets
30 ml/2 tbsp dark soy sauce
4–5 dried Chinese mushrooms
15 ml/1 tbsp dried shrimps
150 g/5 oz glutinous rice
200 ml/7 fl oz boiling water
50 g/2 oz bamboo shoots
100 g/4 oz cooked ham
15 ml/1 tbsp vegetable oil
2–3 spring onions, finely chopped
2 slices ginger root, finely chopped
2.5 ml/½ tsp salt
30–45 ml/2–3 tbsp Shao Hsing rice wine or dry sherry
15 ml/1 tbsp light soy sauce

◆

1 Clean the duck well, reserving the gizzard, and cut off the wings; pat dry inside and out. Brush the skin with soy sauce and leave to dry.
2 Soak the mushrooms and shrimps in warm water for 25–30 minutes.
3 Cook the rice in the water (see p.110).
4 Squeeze the mushrooms dry, discarding the hard stalks, then cut into small cubes.
5 Rinse and drain the shrimps.
6 Place the duck gizzard in a small bowl of boiling water and cook on HIGH for 4–5 minutes; drain and cut into small cubes.
7 Dice the bamboo shoots and ham.
8 Heat the oil in a medium bowl on HIGH for 30–40 seconds, stir in the spring onions and ginger and cook for 1 minute.
9 Add the mushrooms, shrimps, gizzard, bamboo shoots and ham, cook for 2 minutes, then add the salt, soy sauce and wine, mix well and cook for 1 minute.
10 Add the cooked rice and mix well. Pack the stuffing into the body cavity of the duck. Weigh and calculate the cooking time based on 7–9 minutes per 450 g/1 lb. Place the duck breast-side down on a roasting rack, put both inside a large roasting bag and fold the open end lightly underneath.
11 Cook on HIGH for half the calculated cooking time, then remove from the roasting bag and pour off any fat. Turn the duck breast-side uppermost, and complete cooking on the rack uncovered.
12 Remove the duck, cover loosely with foil, and leave to stand for 10 minutes.
13 Scrape out the stuffing and place in a serving bowl. The duck may be carved or chopped into bite-size pieces (see p.8).

BOILED DUCK PEKING-STYLE

◆

2 kg/4½–4¾ lb duckling
2–3 slices ginger root, peeled
2–3 spring onions, cut into short lengths
60 ml/4 tbsp Shao Hsing rice wine or dry sherry
15 ml/1 tbsp salt
15 ml/1 tbsp Sichuan peppercorns

◆

1 Clean the duck well and calculate the cooking time based on 7–9 minutes per 450 g/1 lb. Place the duck in a large casserole, breast-side down, cover with boiling water and cook on HIGH under a vented lid, turning once.
2 Remove the duck, reserving the liquid. Remove all the meat.
3 Place the duck meat in a small casserole, add the ginger, spring onions, wine, salt, pepper and about 150 ml/¼ pt of the cooking liquid. Cover and cook on HIGH for 3–4 minutes. Stand for 10–15 minutes.
4 Remove the duck meat and cut into thin slices or strips. Strain the juice and pour over duck.

M EAT

PORK IS UNDOUBTEDLY THE MOST *widely-eaten meat in China. In fact, for the majority of the Chinese, 'meat' and 'pork' are synonymous. Only 1 per cent of the population (10–11 million people, consisting of Muslims, Mongols, Manchus and the inhabitants of the north-west province, Xinjiang) eat mainly beef, lamb or mutton.*

Like chicken, pork is extremely versatile and lends itself to a wide range of cooking methods. Its mild flavour and neutral savouriness enable it to be combined and cross-cooked with a wider variety of ingredients than lamb, beef or duck.

The Chinese practice of cutting meat into small, thin and neat pieces for the majority of recipes is also the ideal way of preparing meat for the microwave. High heat and short cooking times help to preserve the natural flavours and subtle textures with a minimal loss of nutrients.

MU-SHU PORK WITH EGGS

A bright yellow flower called mu-shu *lends its name to this northern Chinese dish which is also yellow. Traditionally used as a filling in thin pancakes (like Roast Duck Peking-Style on p.85), Mu-Shu Pork can also be wrapped inside lettuce leaves, or served on its own.*

◆

15 g/½ oz wood ears (black fungus)
175–225 g/6–8 oz pork fillet or steak
225 g/8 oz cabbage or leeks
3–4 eggs
5 ml/1 tsp salt
30 ml/2 tbsp oil
2 spring onions, thinly shredded
15 ml/1 tbsp light soy sauce
15 ml/1 tbsp Shao Hsing rice wine or dry sherry
5 ml/1 tsp sesame seed oil

◆

1 Soak the wood ears in warm water for 25–30 minutes.
2 Cut the pork in matchstick-sized shreds.
3 Thinly shred the cabbage or leeks.
4 Rinse the wood ears and cut into thin shreds.
5 Lightly beat the eggs with salt.
6 Heat about half the oil in a small bowl on HIGH for 1 minute, stir in the eggs and cook on HIGH for 1–2 minutes, or until just set, stirring once or twice. Remove.
7 Heat the remaining oil in a casserole, add the pork and cook on HIGH for 1–2 minutes, or until the colour changes, stirring once.
8 Add the cabbage, wood ears, spring onions, salt, soy sauce and wine; mix well and continue cooking for 3–4 minutes on HIGH, stirring once or twice.
9 Stir in the scrambled eggs, breaking them into shreds too. When all the ingredients are well mixed, sprinkle with the sesame seed oil and serve hot.

Left: Kidney 'Flowers' with Vegetables (page 92); *centre:* Mu-shu Pork with Eggs; *right:*
Peking Pancakes (page 113)

KIDNEY 'FLOWERS' WITH VEGETABLES

Originally from Shandong, this recipe is one of my favourites. Some people dislike the strong flavour of kidneys, but if you remove the fat and tough white parts in the middle before cooking, you will find kidneys have a most delicate taste.

◆

15 g/½ oz wood ears (black fungus)
225–275 g/8–10 oz pigs' kidneys
5 ml/1 tsp salt
10 ml/2 tsp cornflour mixed with 15 ml/1 tbsp cold water
5–6 water chestnuts
115 g/4 oz bamboo shoots
115 g/4 oz seasonal greens, such as cabbage, lettuce or spinach
30–45 ml/2–3 tbsp vegetable oil
1 clove garlic, crushed
1 spring onion, finely chopped
5 ml/1 tsp finely chopped ginger root
10 ml/2 tsp vinegar
15 ml/1 tbsp soy sauce
15 ml/1 tbsp Shao Hsing rice wine or dry sherry

◆

1 Soak the wood ears in warm water for 25–30 minutes.
2 Split the kidneys in half lengthways and discard the tough, white parts in the middle. Score about two-thirds of the way through the surface of the kidneys in a fine criss-cross pattern, then cut into pieces the size of oblong postage stamps; when cooked they will open up and resemble ears of corn or 'flowers'.
3 Mix the kidney pieces with a pinch of salt and about half the cornflour paste.
4 Thinly slice the water chestnuts and bamboo shoots.
5 Rinse the wood ears and discard the hard parts.
6 Cover the greens with boiling water and cook for 1–2 minutes on HIGH; remove and drain.

7 Heat the oil in a small casserole, add the garlic, spring onions and ginger to flavour the oil, then add the kidney, cover and cook on HIGH for 2–3 minutes, stirring.
8 Stir in the vinegar followed by the vegetables, salt, soy sauce and wine. Mix well, cover and cook for 1½–2 minutes.
9 Add the remaining cornflour paste, mix well and cook on MEDIUM for 40–50 seconds, stirring once. Serve hot.

BEEF WITH GINGER AND ONIONS

In China onions are known as 'foreign' onions, indicating that their origin is quite different from the native spring onions.

◆

225–275 g/8–10 oz beef steak
15 ml/1 tbsp light soy sauce
2.5 ml/½ tsp ground Sichuan pepper
15 ml/1 tbsp Shao Hsing rice wine or dry sherry
5 ml/1 tsp cornflour mixed with a little water
1 large or 2 medium onions
30 ml/2 tbsp vegetable oil
2–3 slices ginger root, peeled and thinly shredded
2.5 ml/½ tsp salt
a few drops of sesame seed oil

◆

1 Cut the beef into thin strips the size of potato chips.
2 Mix the meat with the soy sauce, pepper, wine and add the cornflour paste. Marinate for 25–30 minutes.
3 Peel and thinly slice the onions.
4 Heat the oil in a small casserole with the ginger and onions for 2–3 minutes on HIGH, or until the onions become translucent.
5 Stir in the beef and salt, cover and cook on HIGH for 2–3 minutes, stirring once or twice. Sprinkle with the sesame seed oil and serve hot.

'LIONS' HEADS'

This dish of pork meat balls braised with cabbage gets its name because the meat balls are supposed to resemble the shape of a lion's head, and the cabbage is supposed to look like its mane. Chinese children (of all ages) love this dish – indeed, it is a great favourite of mine!

◆

450 g/1 lb lean pork, coarsely minced
50 g/2 oz pork fat, finely chopped
225 g/8 oz crabmeat, coarsely chopped
2 spring onions, finely chopped
5 ml/1 tsp finely chopped ginger root
30–45 ml/2–3 tbsp Shao Hsing rice wine or dry sherry
10 ml/2 tsp sugar
30 ml/2 tbsp light soy sauce
15 ml/1 tbsp cornflour
5 ml/1 tsp salt
675 g/1½ lb Chinese leaves, quartered lengthways
30 ml/2 tbsp vegetable oil
85 ml/3 fl oz stock

◆

1 Mix the pork and fat with the crabmeat; add the spring onions, ginger, wine, sugar, soy sauce, cornflour and half the salt, mix well and shape the mixture into 4–6 large round balls.

2 Cut the Chinese leaves into chunks. Place in a large casserole, add the oil and remaining salt and cook on HIGH for 2–3 minutes, or until slightly soft.

3 Place the meatballs on the cabbage and pour the stock over the top. Cook under a vented cover on HIGH for 13–15 minutes. Serve hot.

TWICE-COOKED PORK SICHUAN-STYLE

This is another Sichuan dish that has become popular not only in the rest of China, but throughout the world as well. Any leftovers from Crystal-Boiled Pork (see p.32) can be used in this recipe instead of fresh meat.

◆

225–275 g/8–10 oz leg of pork, boned but not skinned
1 small green pepper, cored and seeded
115 g/4 oz bamboo shoots
25 ml/1½ tbsp vegetable oil
2 spring onions, cut into short lengths
2.5 ml/½ tsp salt
2.5 ml/½ tsp sugar
15 ml/1 tbsp chilli bean paste
15 ml/1 tbsp Shao Hsing rice wine or dry sherry

◆

1 Place the whole piece of pork in a small casserole, cover it with boiling water and a vented lid, then cook on HIGH for 1 minute until boiling again; continue cooking on MEDIUM for 8–10 minutes.

2 Leave the meat in the liquid in the covered casserole for at least 2–3 hours before removing it to cool with the skin-side up.

3 Skin the pork, trimming off some of the excess fat if you are calorie-conscious; slice the meat into thin pieces about the size of a large postage stamp.

4 Cut green pepper and bamboo shoots into small slices.

5 Heat the oil with the spring onions in a small casserole for about 1 minute, then add the green peppers, bamboo shoots, salt, sugar, pork, chilli bean paste and wine. Mix well and cook on HIGH for 3–4 minutes, stirring once or twice. Serve hot.

Bottom left: Cha Shao Pork; *top centre:* Sweet and Sour Pork (page 96); *right:* Perfect Rice (page 112)

CHA SHAO PORK

◆

900 g/2 lb fillet of pork
30 ml/2 tbsp honey dissolved with a little water
lettuce or Chinese leaves
Marinade
2.5 ml/½ tsp salt
15 ml/1 tbsp sugar
15 ml/1 tbsp crushed yellow bean paste
30 ml/2 tbsp Chinese spirit, or brandy, whisky or rum
15 ml/1 tbsp light soy sauce
30 ml/2 tbsp dark soy sauce or Hoi Sin sauce
5 ml/1 tsp sesame seed oil

◆

1 Cut the pork into strips measuring about 18 × 4 × 2.5 cm/7 × 1½ × 1 in. Score the meat on both sides in a diamond pattern.
2 Mix the marinade ingredients in a shallow dish, add the meat, cover and marinate for 12–24 hours.
3 Drain the meat, reserving the marinade. Place the meat on a roasting rack a in single layer and cook on HIGH for 4–5 minutes; rearrange the meat, baste with the marinade and continue cooking for a further 4–5 minutes.
4 Remove the meat from the oven, let it cool down for 2–3 minutes, then brush the strips with honey and place them under a preheated grill for 2–3 minutes, or until they turn a rich golden colour with slightly charred edges.
5 Cut the strips into slices across the grain and arrange them neatly on a bed of lettuce or Chinese leaves.
6 Bring the marinade to the boil in a small jug on HIGH (about 1–2 minutes), stirring once; pour evenly over the meat.
Note Any leftovers will keep in the refrigerator for 4–5 days if stored in an airtight container; for the best flavour and to preserve the moist texture of the meat, try to keep the strips whole and slice just before serving.

SWEET AND SOUR PORK

Without a doubt, this is one of the best-known dishes served in Chinese restaurants, but unfortunately, it is often spoiled by cooks adding too much tomato ketchup to the sauce. Here I have adapted an authentic Cantonese recipe.

◆

275 g/10 oz pork, not too lean
2.5 ml/½ tsp salt
15 ml/1 tbsp brandy, rum or whisky
10 ml/2 tsp cornflour
115 g/4 oz bamboo shoots
1 small green pepper, cored and seeded
30 ml/2 tbsp vegetable oil
1 egg, lightly beaten
15 ml/1 tbsp plain flour
1 clove garlic, crushed and finely chopped
1 spring onion, cut into short lengths
1 small hot chilli, seeded and thinly shredded
(optional)
Sauce
30 ml/2 tbsp vinegar
30 ml/2 tbsp sugar
15 ml/1 tbsp soy sauce
15 ml/1 tbsp tomato paste
10 ml/2 tsp cornflour mixed with 30 ml/2 tbsp water

◆

1 Cut the meat into small cubes not much bigger than the size of olives.
2 Mix together the meat, salt and spirit. Add the cornflour and marinate for about 1 hour.
3 Cut the bamboo shoots and green pepper into small pieces about the same size as the pork.
4 Heat the oil in a preheated browning dish for 1–1½ minutes.
5 Make a light batter with the beaten egg and flour, mix with the pork pieces and cook in the hot dish on HIGH for 2–3 minutes, turning once. Remove and drain.
6 Add the garlic, spring onions, green pepper and bamboo shoots to the browning dish, stir and cook for about 1 minute,

then transfer to a small casserole.
7 Mix the sauce ingredients together, add to the casserole, cover and cook on HIGH for 1–2 minutes, or until bubbling, stirring frequently to make it smooth.
8 Add the pork, stirring well, until each piece of meat is coated with the translucent sauce; cook on MEDIUM for 2–3 minutes, stirring once or twice. Serve immediately.

SHREDDED PORK WITH BEANSPROUTS

The pork in this recipe can be interchanged with chicken or another kind of meat, but you should use only fresh beansprouts.

◆

225 g/8 oz fresh beansprouts
115–175 g/4–6 oz pork fillet
15–30 ml/1–2 tbsp vegetable oil
1–2 spring onions, thinly shredded
15 ml/1 tbsp light soy sauce
15 ml/1 tbsp Shao Hsing rice wine or dry sherry
2.5 ml/½ tsp sugar
2.5 ml/½ tsp salt

◆

1 Wash and rinse the beansprouts, discarding any husks.
2 Thinly shred the pork into strips as fine as the sprouts.
3 Heat about half the oil in a casserole and add the spring onions and pork. Stir to separate the pork shreds, add the soy sauce and wine, mix well and cook on HIGH for 2–3 minutes, or until the meat changes colour.
4 Add the beansprouts, sugar, salt and remaining oil, mix well and cook for 2–3 minutes on HIGH, stirring once or twice. The dish is ready when the beansprouts start to appear transparent and the juice begins to bubble. It should be served immediately.

SPICY DICED PORK

One of the most popular ways of cooking bamboo shoots in China is to quick-braise them with meat.

◆

2.5 ml/½ tsp sugar
15–30 ml/1–2 tbsp Shao Hsing rice wine or dry sherry
15 ml/1 tbsp vegetable oil
30 ml/2 tbsp light soy sauce
450 g/1 lb pork fillet, diced
225 g/8 oz bamboo shoots
2.5 ml/½ tsp five-spice powder
15 ml/1 tbsp chilli bean paste

◆

1 Mix the pork with the sugar, wine, a little of the oil and about half the soy sauce. Marinate for at least 10–15 minutes.
2 Cut the bamboo shoots into small cubes about the same size as the pork.
3 Heat the remaining oil in a small casserole on HIGH for 35–40 seconds, stir in the pork, cover with a vented lid and cook on HIGH for 2–3 minutes, stirring once or twice.
4 Add the bamboo shoots, five-spice powder, chilli bean paste and the remaining soy sauce; mix well, cover with a vented lid and continue cooking on HIGH for 3–4 minutes, stirring once or twice. Serve immediately.

SICHUAN 'KUNG-PO' KIDNEY

A hot and sour version of the kidney 'flowers' recipe from Sichuan.

◆

400 g/14 oz pigs' kidneys
2.5 ml/½ tsp salt
1.25 ml/¼ tsp ground Sichuan pepper
15 ml/1 tbsp Shao Hsing rice wine or dry sherry
5 ml/1 tsp cornflour mixed with 10 ml/2 tsp water
3–4 dried red chillies, seeded and chopped
2–3 spring onions, cut into short lengths
1 clove garlic, crushed and finely chopped
2 slices ginger root, peeled and chopped
30 ml/2 tbsp vegetable oil
a few drops of sesame seed oil
Sauce
15 ml/1 tbsp soy sauce
15 ml/1 tbsp vinegar
15 ml/1 tbsp sugar
45–60 ml/3–4 tbsp stock or water
10 ml/2 tsp cornflour

◆

1 Prepare the kidneys in the same way as on p.92.
2 Mix the kidneys with the salt, pepper and wine, add the cornflour paste and marinate for 10–15 minutes.
3 Mix the sauce ingredients together in a bowl or jug.
4 Heat the oil in a small casserole for about 1 minute, add the chillies, garlic, spring onions and ginger, then stir in the kidney; cover and cook on HIGH for 2–3 minutes, stirring once or twice.
5 Add the sauce, mix well, cover and continue cooking on HIGH for 1–2 minutes, or until the sauce starts to bubble. Add the sesame seed oil and serve hot.

Left: Lamb Slices with Leeks (page 101); *top centre:* Beef with Ginger and Onions (page 92);
right: Stir-fried Pork with Seasonal Greens

STIR-FRIED PORK WITH SEASONAL GREENS

You can use any fresh, young vegetables in this recipe, depending on seasonal availability: mange-tout, broccoli, green peppers, Chinese leaves, green cabbage, asparagus, green beans or courgettes all work equally well.

◆

225 g/8 oz lean pork (fillet or steak)
15 ml/1 tbsp light soy sauce
15 ml/1 tbsp Shao Hsing rice wine or dry sherry
10 ml/2 tsp cornflour mixed with 15 ml/1 tbsp water
30 ml/2 tbsp vegetable oil
225 g/8 oz mange-tout, or any other green vegetable
1–2 spring onions, cut into short lengths
1 slice ginger root, peeled and chopped
2.5 ml/½ tsp salt
2.5 ml/½ tsp sugar

◆

1 Cut the pork into thin slices about the size of an oblong postage stamp.
2 Mix the pork with the soy sauce and wine, add the cornflour paste and about 5 ml/1 tsp oil and leave to marinate for at least 10–15 minutes.
3 Top and tail the mange-tout, leave whole if small, but snap larger ones in half. (Prepare other vegetables as necessary and cut into small slices or pieces about the same size as the pork.)
4 Heat the oil in a small casserole with the spring onions and ginger on HIGH for 1–1½ minutes, stir in the pork, cover with a vented lid and cook on HIGH for 2–3 minutes, or until the meat changes colour, stirring once or twice.
5 Add the mange-tout, or whatever greens you are using, with the salt and sugar, stir well, cover with a vented lid and continue cooking on HIGH for 3–4 minutes, or until just done, stirring once or twice. Serve hot.
Note Do not overcook, or the meat will be tough and the vegetables soggy.

'FISH-FRAGRANT' SHREDDED PORK

The name of this popular dish from Sichuan is a literal translation of yu xiang, *sometimes rendered as 'fish-flavoured' or 'sea-spiced'. But, although the seasonings used for the sauce are exactly those used for cooking a fish dish, no fish is actually used in the recipe.*

◆

25 g/1 oz wood ears (black fungus)
275–350 g/10–12 oz pork fillet
5 ml/1 tsp salt
15 ml/1 tbsp cornflour mixed with 15 ml/1 tbsp water
2–3 stalks celery hearts or young leeks
30 ml/2 tbsp oil
1 clove garlic, crushed and finely chopped
5 ml/1 tsp finely chopped ginger root
2 spring onions, finely chopped
15 ml/1 tbsp soy sauce
15 ml/1 tbsp chilli bean paste
2.5 ml/½ tsp sugar
10 ml/2 tsp vinegar

◆

1 Soak the wood ears for 25–30 minutes.
2 Cut the pork into matchstick-sized shreds, then mix with a little salt and about half the cornflour paste.
3 Thinly shred the celery or leeks.
4 Rinse the wood ears, discard the hard parts and cut into thin shreds.
5 Heat about half the oil with the garlic, ginger and spring onions in a small casserole on HIGH for about 1 minute; stir in the pork, cover with a vented lid and cook on HIGH for 2–3 minutes, or until the pork changes colour, stirring once or twice.
6 Stir in the celery or leeks, wood ears, salt, soy sauce, chilli bean paste, sugar, vinegar and the remaining oil. Mix well, cover with a vented lid and continue cooking on HIGH for 2–3 minutes, stirring.
7 Add the remaining cornflour paste, mix well and cook on MEDIUM for 40–50 seconds.

SLICED BEEF IN OYSTER SAUCE

To a Chinese palate, beef always tastes a trifle strong and tough compared with pork, so we often cook it with plenty of seasonings and spices. Oyster sauce is a Cantonese speciality, and the main feature of this dish is its extreme savouriness and tenderness.

◆

275–350 g/10–12 oz beef steak
2.5 ml/½ tsp sugar
15 ml/1 tbsp light soy sauce
15 ml/1 tbsp Shao Hsing rice wine or dry sherry
10 ml/2 tsp cornflour mixed with a little water
1 small head Chinese leaves or cos lettuce
30 ml/2 tbsp vegetable oil
2 spring onions, cut into short lengths
1 slice ginger root, peeled and chopped
2.5 ml/½ tsp salt
30 ml/2 tbsp oyster sauce

◆

1 Cut the beef into thin slices about the size of a large postage stamp.
2 Mix the meat the sugar, soy sauce and wine, add the cornflour paste and marinate for at least 1–2 hours. (The longer the marinating, the more tender the beef will be.)
3 Separate and wash the Chinese leaves or lettuce and cut each leaf into 2 or 3 pieces.
4 Heat the oil in a casserole with the spring onions and ginger root on HIGH for about 1 minute; add the chopped leaves and salt, then cook on HIGH for 2–3 minutes, or until the leaves are limp, stirring once or twice.
5 Add the beef and oyster sauce, mix well and continue cooking on HIGH for 2–3 minutes, stirring once or twice. (Do not overcook, or you will toughen the beef.) Serve immediately.

LAMB SLICES WITH LEEKS

A very popular dish served in good Peking restaurants. The lamb must be cut into very thin slices and cooked in the shortest possible time.

◆

15 g/½ oz wood ears (black fungus)
275–350 g/10–12 oz leg of lamb fillet
3–4 spring onions
15 ml/1 tbsp light soy sauce
15 ml/1 tbsp Shao Hsing rice wine or dry sherry
10 ml/2 tsp cornflour mixed with a little water
5 ml/1 tsp sesame seed oil
1–2 young leeks
30 ml/2 tbsp vegetable oil
1 clove garlic, crushed
2.5 ml/½ tsp salt
2.5 ml/½ tsp sugar
15 ml/1 tbsp crushed yellow bean sauce
5 ml/1 tsp vinegar

◆

1 Soak the wood ears in warm water for 25–30 minutes.
2 Trim off the excess fat from the lamb and cut into small slices as thin as possible.
3 Cut the spring onions in half lengthways, then slice them diagonally.
4 Mix the lamb and onions with the soy sauce and wine, add the cornflour paste and sesame seed oil and marinate for at least 2–3 hours.
5 Wash the leeks well and cut into small slices.
6 Rinse the wood ears and discard the hard parts.
7 Heat the oil with the garlic in a small casserole on HIGH for about 1 minute; add the leeks, wood ears, salt, sugar and bean paste, mix well, cover and cook on HIGH for 1–2 minutes.
8 Stir in the lamb, add the vinegar, cover and continue cooking on HIGH for 2–3 minutes, or until done, stirring once or twice. Serve immediately.

DICED LAMB IN PEKING SWEET BEAN SAUCE

It is said that this is the original sweet and sour dish, from the Yellow River valley in north China.

◆

275–350 g/10–12 oz leg of lamb fillet
15 ml/1 tbsp brandy, rum or whisky
15 ml/1 tbsp crushed yellow bean sauce
10 ml/2 tsp cornflour
½ cucumber
30 ml/2 tbsp vegetable oil
5 ml/1 tsp finely chopped ginger root
2.5 ml/½ tsp sesame seed oil
Sauce
15 ml/1 tbsp soy sauce
15 ml/1 tbsp Shao Hsing rice wine or dry sherry
15 ml/1 tbsp vinegar
30 ml/2 tbsp sugar
15 ml/1 tbsp cornflour mixed with 45 ml/3 tbsp stock or water

◆

1 Trim off the excess fat from the lamb, then dice the meat into small cubes the size of sugar lumps.
2 Mix the meat with the alcohol and yellow bean sauce, add the cornflour paste and marinate for at least 30–40 minutes.
3 Wash but do not peel the cucumber, then cut it into small cubes about the same size as the lamb.
4 Mix the sauce ingredients together in a bowl or jug.
5 Heat the oil in a preheated browning dish for about 1 minute, add the lamb, stir to separate and cook on HIGH for 2–3 minutes, or until the meat changes colour.
6 Transfer the meat to a small casserole, add the ginger, cucumber and sauce mixture, mix well, cover and cook on HIGH for 2–3 minutes, stirring once or twice. Serve immediately.

RED-COOKED BEEF WITH TOMATOES

As food is cooked so quickly in a microwave oven, tough cuts of beef do not have time to become tender, so it is best to use a slightly more expensive cut of meat.

◆

675 g/1½ lb braising steak or topside beef
45 ml/3 tbsp Shao Hsing rice wine or dry sherry
2–3 spring onions, cut into short lengths
2–3 slices ginger root, peeled and crushed
450 g/1 lb tomatoes, halved or quartered
30 ml/2 tbsp light soy sauce
15 ml/1 tbsp dark soy sauce
85 g/3 oz crystallized or rock sugar
10 ml/2 tsp cornflour mixed with a little water
salt and pepper to taste

◆

1 Cut the beef into 2.5 cm/1 in cubes, trimming off any excess fat.
2 Place the meat in a casserole, add the wine, spring onions, ginger, tomatoes, soy sauce and about 150 ml/¼ pt water. Cover with a vented lid and cook on HIGH for 4–5 minutes, or until boiling, stirring once. Continue cooking on LOW for 30 minutes, stirring once or twice.
3 Add the sugar and cook on HIGH for 4–5 minutes.
4 Thicken the liquid with the cornflour paste and cook on HIGH for 30–40 seconds. Adjust the seasoning and serve hot.

Left: Beef and Green Peppers in Black Bean Sauce (page 104); *bottom right:* Sliced Beef in Oyster Sauce (page 100); *top right: Red-cooked Beef with Tomatoes*

BARBECUE PORK SPARE-RIBS

Most pork spare-ribs contain a great deal of fat which causes the barbecue to flame during cooking, so you often end up with a pile of charred ribs that are underdone inside. One way of avoiding this is to pre-cook the spare-ribs in a microwave oven, then crisp them on the barbecue to acquire that slightly charred look.

◆

900 g/2 lb pork spare-ribs
Marinade
2 cloves garlic, crushed
2 slices ginger root, crushed
45 ml/3 tbsp crushed yellow bean paste, or 45 ml/3 tbsp soy sauce mixed with 15 ml/1 tbsp cornflour
15 ml/1 tbsp sugar
15 ml/1 tbsp vinegar
30–45 ml/2–3 tbsp Shao Hsing rice wine or dry sherry
5 ml/1 tsp chilli sauce
5 ml/1 tsp sesame seed oil

◆

1 Trim off the excess fat and gristle from the meat and cut into individual ribs.
2 Mix the marinade ingredients in a shallow dish, add the meat, cover and marinate for 4–6 hours, turning several times.
3 Cook the spare-ribs in the marinade on HIGH for 10–12 minutes, turning them over halfway through. When done, remove the ribs from the liquid to cool a little.
4 Barbecue the ribs on a hot grid for about 5 minutes, turning them frequently and basting with the sauce. Serve hot.

BEEF AND GREEN PEPPERS IN BLACK BEAN SAUCE

Although this is a Cantonese dish, both Peking and Sichuan restaurants have it on their menus.

◆

225–275 g/8–10 oz beef steak
15 ml/1 tbsp soy sauce
15 ml/1 tbsp Shao Hsing rice wine or dry sherry
2.5 ml/½ tsp sugar
5 ml/1 tsp cornflour mixed with a little water
1 large or 2 small green peppers, cored and seeded
1 large or 2 small onions
30 ml/2 tbsp vegetable oil
2 spring onions, cut into short lengths
1 slice ginger root, peeled and chopped
1–2 green or red hot chillies, seeded and thinly sliced
30 ml/2 tbsp crushed black bean sauce

◆

1 Cut the beef into thin slices about the size of a large postage stamp.
2 Mix the meat with the soy sauce, wine and sugar. Add the cornflour paste and marinate for 25–30 minutes.
3 Cut the green peppers and onions into pieces the same size as the beef.
4 Heat the oil with the spring onions, ginger and chillies in a small casserole on HIGH for about 1 minute. Add the green pepper, onions and the black bean sauce, mix well and cook on HIGH for 1–2 minutes, stirring once.
5 Add the beef, mix well and continue cooking on HIGH for 2–3 minutes, stirring once or twice. Serve hot.

'MA-PO' BEAN CURD WITH MINCED MEAT

Ma-Po was the wife of a Sichuan chef who worked in the provincial capital, Chengdu, about 100 years ago. This universally popular dish has a number of variations: some Cantonese restaurants list is as 'Spicy and Hot Bean Curd' or simply as 'Sichuan Bean Curd'.

◆

3 cakes bean curd
1 leek or 3–4 spring onions
15 ml/1 tbsp salted black beans, crushed
15 ml/1 tbsp Shao Hsing rice wine or dry sherry
30 ml/2 tbsp oil
1 clove garlic, finely chopped
115 g/4 oz lean pork, beef or lamb, coarsely chopped
15 ml/1 tbsp chilli bean paste
2.5 ml/½ tsp sugar
15 ml/1 tbsp soy sauce
50 ml/2 fl oz stock
10 ml/2 tsp cornflour mixed with a little cold water
ground Sichuan pepper

◆

1 Cut the bean curd into 1 cm/½ in cubes, cover with boiling water and cook on HIGH for 2 minutes; remove and drain.
2 Cut the leek or onions into short lengths.
3 Mix the salted black beans with the wine.
4 Heat the oil in a small casserole for about 1 minute, then add the garlic to flavour the oil for 30–40 seconds. Stir in the meat, cover and cook on HIGH for about 2 minutes, or until the colour changes.
5 Add the chilli bean paste and black bean mixture; stir well.
6 Add the leek or spring onions, bean curd, sugar, soy sauce and stock, cover and cook on HIGH for 2–3 minutes.
7 Stir in the cornflour paste to thicken the liquid, mix well and cook on MEDIUM for 40–50 seconds, stirring once very gently. Serve hot sprinkled with the pepper.

HUNAN BRAISED BEAN CURD FAMILY-STYLE

Of the eight provinces that border Sichuan, only Hunan to the south-east is closely affiliated with the cooking of its distinguished neighbour – they both like hot and spicy food.

◆

4 cakes bean curd
115 g/4 oz lean pork
30 ml/2 tbsp vegetable oil
2.5 ml/½ tsp salt
2 spring onions, cut into short lengths
3–4 fresh or dried red chillies, seeded and chopped
15 ml/1 tbsp bean paste
15 ml/1 tbsp soy sauce
10 ml/2 tsp cornflour mixed with a little water
a few drops of sesame seed oil

◆

1 Split each cake of bean curd crossways into 3 or 4 thin slices, then cut each slice diagonally into 2 triangles.
2 Cut the pork into small, thin slices.
3 Heat the oil in a preheated browning dish for about 1 minute and fry the bean curd triangles on HIGH for 2–3 minutes, or until golden on both sides.
4 Transfer the bean curd to a small casserole, add the pork, salt, spring onions, chillies, bean paste and soy sauce; stir very gently, cover and cook for 3–4 minutes, stirring very gently once or twice.
5 Stir in the cornflour paste to thicken the liquid and cook on MEDIUM for 40–50 seconds, stirring once. Add the sesame seed oil and serve hot.

Top left: Pork Slices with Bamboo Shoots and Chinese Mushrooms; *top right:* Singapore-style Fried Rice Noodles (page 113); *bottom:* Shredded Pork with Bean Sprouts (page 96)

LIVER SLICES AND WOOD EARS

The contrast between the crunchiness of the fungus and the tender softness of the liver makes this dish extremely popular. Never overcook liver or the delicate texture will be ruined.

◆

25 g/1 oz wood ears (black fungus)
275–350 g/10–12 oz pigs' liver
2–3 spring onions, cut into short lengths
30 ml/2 tbsp vegetable oil
15 ml/1 tbsp light soy sauce
5 ml/1 tsp cornflour mixed with a little water
salt and pepper

◆

1 Soak the wood ears in warm water for 25–30 minutes.
2 Wash the liver and pat dry; discard the white membranes, then cut the liver into thin matchbox-sized pieces.
3 Place the liver in a large bowl, cover with boiling water, stir to separate each piece then drain through a sieve; mix the liver with the soy sauce and cornflour paste.
4 Heat the oil in a small casserole on HIGH for 1–2 minutes.
5 Meanwhile, rinse the wood ears, discarding the hard parts, then tear large ones into small pieces.
6 Stir the liver into the hot oil, then add the spring onions, wood ears, salt and pepper. Cover and cook on HIGH for 2–3 minutes, or until done, stirring once or twice. Serve hot.

PORK SLICES WITH BAMBOO SHOOTS AND CHINESE MUSHROOMS

Another name for this delicious dish from Shanghai is Stir-Fried Pork with 'Two Winters', the 'two winters' being winter bamboo shoots and winter mushrooms.

◆

6–8 dried Chinese mushrooms
225g/8 oz pork fillet
15 ml/1 tbsp light soy sauce
15 ml/1 tbsp Shao Hsing rice wine or dry sherry
15 ml/1 tbsp cornflour mixed with 15 ml/1 tbsp cold water
225–275 g/8–10 oz winter bamboo shoots
30 ml/2 tbsp vegetable oil
5 ml/1 tsp salt
2.5 ml/½ tsp sugar
2.5 ml/½ tsp sesame seed oil

◆

1 Soak the mushrooms in warm water for 20–25 minutes.
2 Cut the pork into thin slices about the size of a postage stamp.
3 Stir the meat into the soy sauce and wine and then add about one-third of the cornflour paste. Allow to marinate for at least 10–15 minutes.
4 Squeeze dry the mushrooms and discard the hard stalks; halve or quarter the mushrooms, depending on their size.
5 Drain the bamboo shoots and cut into thin slices the same size as the pork.
6 Heat the oil in a small casserole, add the pork and cook on HIGH for about 2–3 minutes, or until the colour changes, stirring once or twice.
7 Add the mushrooms, bamboo shoots, salt and sugar, mix well and continue cooking on HIGH for 2–3 minutes, stirring once or twice.
8 Add the remaining cornflour paste, stir and cook on MEDIUM for 40–50 seconds. Sprinkle with the seasame seed oil and serve.

RICE NOODLES AND SNACKS

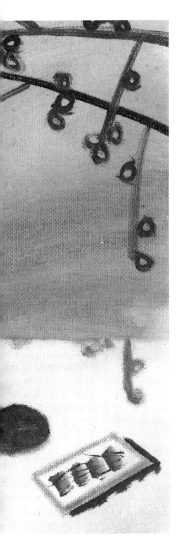

RICE HAS BEEN THE STAPLE *food of most Chinese for centuries. In fact,* fan, *the Chinese word for 'cooked rice', also denotes all the grain and starch content of a meal and can even be used to mean 'meal'. In the past, it was only in the southern half of China, south of the Yangtze River, that rice predominated – people in north China had to rely heavily on wheat products for their everyday meals. But with modern developments in cultivation, plus much improved methods of transport, plain boiled or steamed rice now forms the bulk food for most Chinese people in both north and south. Fried rice and noodles (fried or added to soup) are often served alone as a light meal or snack. Bread is not widely eaten, but we do eat steamed buns, dumplings and pancakes, both sweet and savoury.*

Everyday meals are seldom concluded with a dessert. Most sweet dishes are served either as a snack, or to cleanse the palate between courses on more formal occasions. If you wish to serve something sweet as a dessert, I would suggest fresh fruit, such as kiwi fruit, clementines or kumquats.

CHOW MEIN

Chow Mein *(fried noodles) is be one of the most popular Chinese dishes in the West.*

◆

275 g/10 oz dried egg noodles, or
450 g/1 lb fresh egg noodles
225 g/8 oz chicken breast meat, beef steak or pork fillet, or 115 g/4 oz cooked meat, such as Cha Shao Pork or Fragrant Pork (see pp 95 and 33)
30 ml/2 tbsp vegetable oil
2 spring onions, thinly shredded
115 g/4 oz mange-tout or French beans, topped and tailed
115 g/4 oz peeled prawns
5 ml/1 tsp salt
15−30 ml/1−2 tbsp Shao Hsing rice wine or dry sherry
30 ml/2 tbsp light soy sauce
5 ml/1 tsp sesame seed oil

◆

1 Cook the noodles in a pan of boiling water according to the instructions on the packet; drain and rinse under cold water until cool. (Fresh noodles require far less cooking time than dried, usually needing only to be soaked in boiling water for 1−2 minutes before rinsing in cold water.) Drain and mix with a little oil.

2 Thinly shred the meat. Do not use more than one type for the same dish.

3 Heat the oil in a casserole, add the spring onions, meat, vegetable, prawns, salt and wine, mix well and cook on HIGH for 3−4 minutes, if using fresh meat, or 2−3 minutes, if using cooked meat. Stir once or twice, then remove about half the mixture and keep warm.

4 Add the noodles and soy sauce to the casserole, stir well and continue cooking on HIGH for 1−2 minutes, or until thoroughly heated through. Transfer to a large serving dish, spoon the reserved meat mixture on top and sprinkle with the sesame seed oil. Serve hot or cold.

Left: Chow Mein; *right:* Yangchow Fried Rice (page 112)

YANGCHOW FRIED RICE

The rice to be used for frying should ideally be cold and firm and you can use virtually any permutation of ingredients for flavouring.

◆

350–450 g/12 oz-1 lb cooked rice, or
175–225 g/6–8 oz raw rice
3–4 dried Chinese mushrooms, or 50 g/2 oz fresh button mushrooms
115 g/4 oz cooked chicken, ham, or pork, such as Cha Shao Pork, Crystal-Boiled Pork or Fragrant Pork (see pp 95, 32 and 33)
50 g/2 oz peeled prawns
50 g/2 oz bamboo shoots, or young carrots
2–3 eggs
5 ml/1 tsp salt
2 spring onions, finely chopped
30 ml/2 tbsp vegetable oil
115 g/4 oz peas
15 ml/1 tbsp Shao Hsing rice wine or dry sherry
15 ml/1 tbsp light soy sauce

◆

1 If you have to cook some rice specially for this dish, cook it well in advance and allow it to cool.
2 If using dried mushrooms, soak them in warm water for 20–25 minutes, then squeeze dry, discard the hard stalks and dice into small cubes the size of peas. If using fresh mushrooms, cut them to the same size.
3 Dice the chicken, ham or pork into roughly pea-size cubes.
4 Dice the bamboo shoots or carrots into similar small cubes.
5 Leave the prawns whole if small, otherwise cut each one into 2–3 pieces.
6 Lightly beat the eggs with a pinch of salt and a few bits of finely chopped spring onions.
7 Lightly oil a shallow pie plate, pour in the eggs and cook on HIGH for about 1 minute, or until the edges of the egg are set; lift the cooked egg and allow the uncooked part to flow to the edges of the plate; continue cooking until all the egg is set. Remove and break the omelette into small pieces.
8 Heat the remaining oil in a casserole, add the diced mushrooms, meat, bamboo shoots or carrots, prawns, peas, wine and soy sauce, stir well and cook on HIGH for 2–3 minutes, stirring once.
9 Add the cooked rice, egg, spring onions and salt; stir to make sure that each grain of rice is separate, then cook on HIGH for 1–2 minutes. Serve hot.

PERFECT RICE

There are two main types of rice on sale in the West: long-grain or Patna rice, and round pudding rice. If you like your rice to be firm yet fluffy, use the long-grain type, as round rice tends to be rather soft and stick together when cooked. Allow about 50 g/2 oz raw rice per person, unless you are very hearty eaters.

◆

225 g/8 oz rice
600 ml/1 pt boiling water
1.25 ml/¼ tsp salt

◆

1 Wash and rinse the rice in cold water just once; sometimes this is not necessary when the rice is well packaged.
2 Place the rice in a casserole, add the boiling water and salt, stir once or twice, then cook under a vented lid on HIGH for 12–13 minutes.
3 Stand for 10–12 minutes or so, then fluff the rice up with a fork or spoon before serving.

Note For 450 g/1 lb raw rice, use 900 ml/1½ pt boiling water, and cook for 14–15 minutes. To warm up any leftover cooked rice, add a little cold water and cook on HIGH for 4–5 minutes.

PEKING PANCAKES

Although traditionally served with Peking Duck and Mu-shu Pork (see pp 85 and 90), these pancakes can be used as a wrapper for any dish instead of serving it with rice. They can be made well in advance, frozen (unfilled) and warmed up by steaming for 2–3 minutes before use. The quantities given below make 24–30 pancakes.

◆

450 g/1 lb plain flour
300 ml/½ pt boiling water
5 ml/1 tsp vegetable oil

◆

1 Sift the flour into a mixing bowl, then pour in the boiling water and oil very gently, stirring as you pour.
2 Knead the mixture into a firm dough, cover with a damp towel and leave to stand for about 30 minutes.
3 Lightly dust a work top with flour and knead the dough for about 5–8 minutes, or until smooth.
4 Divide the dough into 3 equal portions and roll each into a long sausage-shape; cut each 'sausage' into 8–10 pieces. Using the palm of your hand, press each piece into a flat pancake.
5 Dust the work top with more flour, flatten each pancake into a 15 cm/6 in circle with a rolling pin, and roll gently on both sides.
6 Place an ungreased frying pan over a high heat. When hot, reduce the heat to low and cook one or two pancakes at a time. Turn over when little brown spots appear on the underside. Remove and keep under a damp cloth until all the pancakes have been cooked.

SINGAPORE-STYLE FRIED RICE NOODLES

◆

Also known as rice-sticks or vermicelli, rice noodles are very popular in southern China, where they are interchangeable with noodles made from wheat flour in most recipes.

◆

15 ml/1 tbsp dried shrimps
275-350 g/10-12 oz rice noodles
115 g/4 oz pork or beef, coarsely chopped
1 medium onion, thinly sliced
115 g/4 oz fresh beansprouts
1 leek, or 2 spring onions, thinly shredded
30 ml/2 tbsp vegetable oil
2.5 ml/½ tsp salt
10 ml/2 tsp curry powder
30 ml/2 tbsp light soy sauce
1 green or red chilli, seeded and thinly shredded
(optional)

◆

1 Soak the shrimps in hot water for 25–30 minutes.
2 Soak the rice noodles in hot water for 10–15 minutes, or until soft. Drain, rinse in cold water and drain again.
3 Wash and rinse the beansprouts.
4 Drain the shrimps.
5 Heat about half the oil in a casserole, add the meat, stir to separate the pieces and cook on HIGH for 2-3 minutes, stirring once.
6 Add the onion, leek or spring onions, shrimps, beansprouts, salt and curry powder, mix well and cook on HIGH for 2–3 minutes, stirring once or twice. Remove and reserve.
7 Put the remaining oil and drained rice noodles in the casserole, stir well to distribute the oil evenly, then add the soy sauce, meat mixture and chilli shreds (if using). Stir well and cook on HIGH for 1–2 minutes. Serve hot or cold.

MENU SELECTION

TO THE WESTERN EYE *and palate used to what is commonly known as the 'Russian service', that is, serving meals in three courses, more or less, ending with a sweet dish, composing Chinese recipes into a balanced meal may seem a mystery. The following pages contain several menu suggestions, from a simple meal for four to a buffet for up to twenty-four.*

MENUS FOR FOUR

——————— 1 ———————

FISH SLICES AND LETTUCE SOUP

SHREDDED CHICKEN WITH CELERY

RED-COOKED BEEF WITH TOMATOES

PLAIN RICE

——————— 2 ———————

BEAN CURD AND SPINACH SOUP

FISH FILLET IN WINE SAUCE PEKING-
STYLE or FILLET OF SOLE WITH
MUSHROOMS

STIR-FRIED PORK WITH SEASONAL
GREENS or BEEF AND GREEN PEPPERS IN
BLACK BEAN SAUCE

PLAIN RICE

——————— 3 ———————

CHICKEN AND HAM SALAD WITH
MUSTARD SAUCE

BRAISED MONKFISH TAILS or FISH STEAK
IN SWEET AND SOUR SAUCE

BARBECUE PORK SPARE RIBS or LIONS
HEADS

QUICK-BRAISED LETTUCE HEART or STIR-
FRIED BEANSPROUTS

PLAIN RICE

——————— 4 ———————

VEGETARIAN

BRAISED CHINESE LEAVES WITH
MUSHROOMS or BRAISED AUBERGINES

BEAN CURD WITH SPINACH or MIXED
VEGETABLES

VEGETARIAN CASSEROLE or STEAMED
CAULIFLOWER IN CREAM SAUCE

◆

MENUS FOR SIX

——————— 1 ———————

CHICKEN AND BEANSPROUT SOUP or
SLICED LAMB AND CUCUMBER SOUP

SHREDDED PORK WITH BEANSPROUTS or
STIR-FRIED PORK WITH SEASONAL GREENS

BRAISED CHICKEN IN BROWN SAUCE or
RED-COOKED CHICKEN

STIR-FRIED GREEN CABBAGE or BRAISED
BRUSSELS SPROUTS

PLAIN RICE

——————— 2 ———————

SOY-BRAISED CHICKEN or SOY-BRAISED
BEEF

SQUID-FLOWERS WITH GREEN PEPPERS

CHICKEN SLICES AND VEGETABLES or
LAMB SLICES WITH LEEKS

STIR FRIED FRENCH BEANS or BRAISED
BROCCOLI IN OYSTER SAUCE

PLAIN RICE

——————— 3 ———————

PRAWNS IN SWEET AND SOUR SAUCE or
FISH STEAK IN SWEET AND SOUR SAUCE

DRUNKEN CHICKEN or STEAMED
CHIICKEN WITH CHINESE MUSHROOMS

SLICED BEEF IN OYSTER SAUCE or BEEF
WITH GINGER AND ONIONS

QUICK-FRY OF 'FOUR PRECIOUS
VEGETABLES' or COURGETTES WITH RED
PEPPERS

PLAIN RICE

—————— 4 ——————

NO MEAT

SEAFOOD AND ASPARAGUS SOUP

FILLET OF SOLE WITH MUSHROOMS or
BRAISED 'TWO WINTERS'

RED-COOKED FISH or BRAISED
AUBERGINES

SEAFOOD CASSEROLE or 'BUDDHAS
DELIGHT' – EIGHT TREASURES OF
CHINESE VEGETABLES

PLAIN RICE

SUGGESTED WINES

WHITE

WHITE – Pouilly Fuisse, Riesling,
Macon Blanc or Californian Chardonnay.

RED – Beaujolais Villages, Spanish
Rioja, Macon Rouge, Bourgogne (Pinot
Noir), St. Emilion or Californian
Cabernet Sauvignon.

MENUS FOR EIGHT TO TEN

—————— 1 ——————

INFORMAL STYLE

KIDNEY AND CELERY SALAD or CHICKEN
AND HAM SALAD WITH MUSTARD SAUCE

GREEN BEANS AND RED PEPPER SALAD or
MIXED VEGETABLE SALAD WITH SPICY
DRESSING

CRYSTAL-BOILED PORK WITH CRUSHED
GARLIC SAUCE or FRAGRANT PORK

PRAWNS IN SWEET AND SOUR SAUCE or
GREEN PEPPERS WITH PRAWN STUFFING

FISH AND BEAN CURD IN HOT AND SOUR
SAUCE or BRAISED FISH IN HOT BEAN
SAUCE

DICED CHICKEN WITH GREEN PEPPERS or
CHICKEN SLICES AND VEGETABLES

MU-SHU PORK WITH EGGS or SLICED BEEF
IN OYSTER SAUCE

MIXED VEGETABLES or 'THREE WHITES' IN
CREAM SAUCE

PLAIN RICE

—————— 2 ——————

SOY-BRAISED CHICKEN or SHANGHAI
SOYA DUCK

EGG FU-YUNG WITH PRAWNS OR
CRABMEAT

CHICKEN CUBES WITH CUCUMBER or
DICED CHICKEN WITH GREEN PEPPERS

PORK SLICES WITH BAMBOO SHOOTS AND
CHINESE MUSHROOMS or KIDNEY
'FLOWERS' WITH VEGETABLES

HUNAN BRAISED BEAN CURD FAMILY-STYLE or *DICED LAMB IN PEKING SWEET BEAN SAUCE*

QUICK-FRIED LETTUCE HEART or *BRAISED CHINESE BROCCOLI*

PLAIN RICE

◆

MENUS FOR TEN TO TWELVE

——— 1 ———

FORMAL STYLE

COLD STARTERS

POACHED PRAWNS PEKING-STYLE

SICHUAN BON-BON CHICKEN

BRAISED TRIPE AND TONGUE

GREEN BEANS AND RED PEPPER SALAD

HOT STARTERS

FISH FILLET IN WINE SAUCE PEKING-STYLE

SICHUAN 'KUNG-PO' CHICKEN WITH CASHEW NUTS

SHREDDED PORK WITH BEAN SPROUTS

MAIN COURSE SERVED WITH RICE

RED-COOKED BEEF WITH TOMATOES

STEAMED FISH IN BLACK BEAN SAUCE CANTON-STYLE

BRAISED BROCCOLI IN OYSTER SAUCE

THREE-FLAVOUR SOUP

——— 2 ———

COLD STARTERS

ASSORTED HORS D'OEUVRES

HOT STARTERS

'CRYSTAL' PRAWNS

CHICKEN SLICES AND VEGETABLES

'FISH-FRAGRANT' SHREDDED PORK

TOMATO AND EGG SCRAMBLE

PRINCIPAL DISH

ROAST DUCK PEKING-STYLE

MAIN COURSE SERVED WITH RICE

EIGHT-TREASURE DUCK

BARBECUE PORK SPARE RIBS

BRAISED WHOLE FISH IN SWEET AND SOUR SAUCE

BRAISED CHINESE LEAVES WITH MUSHROOMS

——— 3 ———

STARTERS

CRYSTAL-BOILED PORK WITH CRUSHED GARLIC SAUCE

PRAWNS WITH SWEET AND SOUR SAUCE

BEANSPROUT SALAD

MAIN COURSE SERVED WITH RICE

SICHUAN PRAWNS WITH GARLIC AND CHILLI SAUCE

CHICKEN FU-YUNG

BEEF AND GREEN PEPPERS IN BLACK BEAN SAUCE

SHREDDED PORK WITH BEAN SPROUTS

BRAISED CHINESE LEAVES WITH MUSHROOMS

FU-YUNG BEAN CURD

SOUP

CHINESE CABBAGE AND MUSHROOM SOUP

◆

BUFFET STYLE FOR SIXTEEN TO TWENTY-FOUR

PRAWNS WITH SWEET AND SOUR SAUCE or *POACHED PRAWNS PEKING STYLE*

LOBSTER CANTONESE IN BLACK BEAN SAUCE or *CRAB WITH SPRING ONIONS AND GINGER*

SOY-BRAISED CHICKEN or *ROAST CHICKEN CANTON-STYLE*

EIGHT-TREASURE DUCK or *BOILED DUCK PEKING-STYLE*

BRAISED WHOLE FISH IN SWEET AND SOUR SAUCE or *RED-COOKED FISH*

CHA SHAO PORK or *CRYSTAL-BOILED PORK WITH CRUSHED GARLIC SAUCE*

SOY-BRAISED BEEF or *BRAISED TRIPE AND TONGUE*

MIXED VEGETABLE SALAD WITH SPICY DRESSING or *GREEN BEANS AND RED PEPPER SALAD*

YANGCHOW FRIED RICE

CHOW MEIN (FRIED NOODLES)

◆

SUGGESTED WINES

As an aperitif as well as to go with the cold starters, serve any light white wine such as: *Muscadet, Graves, Sauvignon, Riesling or Chardonnay.*

For the hot starters, or for those who prefer white wine to red: *try Alsace, Côtes de Rhône Blanc, Pouilly Fume or Chablis.*

Also for the hot starters, serve red wines such as: *Beaujolais, Chinon, Bourgueil or Sancerre Rouge.*

For the main course, a more robust red would be suitable. Try: *St. Emilion, Medoc, Graves (Rouge), Burgundy (Beaune, Volnay etc), Côtes du Rhône, Chateauneuf-du-Pape, Hermitage, Rubesco, Barbaresco, Rioja, Pinot Noir or Cabernet Sauvignon.*

GLOSSARY

Agar agar Also known as Isinglass (*Kanten* in Japanese); a product of seaweed, sold dried in paper-thin strands or powdered form. Gelatine may be substituted.

Bamboo shoots Available in cans only. Once opened, the contents may be kept in fresh water in a covered jar for up to a week in the refrigerator. Try to get *winter bamboo shoots,* which have a firmer texture.

Bean curd Also known as *tofu,* this is a custard-like preparation of puréed and pressed soya beans exceptionally high in protein. It is usually sold in cakes about 7.5 cm/3 in square and 2.5 cm/1 in thick and is available from Oriental and health food stores. It will keep for a few days if submerged in water and stored in the refrigerator.

Beansprouts Fresh beansprouts, from mung or soya beans, are widely available from Oriental stores and most supermarkets. They can be kept in the refrigerator for 2–3 days. Do not overcook them, and never use canned beansprouts as they lack crispness which is their main characteristic.

Bean sauce Available in several varieties. See *Black bean sauce, Chilli bean paste, Hoi Sin sauce, Yellow bean paste.*

Black bean sauce A thick paste made from salted black beans which are crushed and mixed with flour and spices, such as ginger, garlic or chilli. Sold in jars or cans, it should be kept in the refrigerator once opened. Provided it remains untouched by grease, water or other organic substances, it should last almost indefinitely.

Black beans, salted Very salty and pungent, these are sold in plastic bags, jars or cans; they should be crushed with water or wine before use and will keep almost indefinitely in a covered jar.

Chilli bean paste Fermented bean paste mixed with hot chillies and other seasonings. Sold in jars, some are quite mild, but some are very hot. Only trial and error will reveal which variety is to your taste.

Chilli sauce A very hot sauce made from chillies, vinegar, sugar and salt. It is usually sold in bottles and should be used sparingly. Tabasco sauce can be substituted.

Chinese cleaver An all-purpose cook's knife used for slicing, shredding, peeling, pounding, crushing, chopping, and even for transporting cut food from the chopping board to a plate. Chinese cleavers are available in a variety of materials and weights; choose a medium-weight, dual-purpose cleaver known as the 'Civil and military' (*wen-wu dao* in Chinese). It has a blade about 20–23 cm/8–9 in long and 7.5–10 cm/3–4 in wide. Use the lighter, front half of the blade for slicing, shredding and scoring, and the heavier, rear half of the blade for chopping.

Chinese leaves Also known as Chinese cabbage, there are two varieties widely available in supermarkets and greengrocers. The most common one is pale green and has a tight, elongated head; about two-thirds of the cabbage is stem, which has a crunchy texture. The other variety has a shorter and fatter head with curlier, pale yellow or green leaves.

Chinese mushrooms, dried (*Lentinus edodes*) These are highly fragrant dried mushrooms sold in plastic bags; they are not cheap, but a small amount goes a long way and they will keep indefinitely in an airtight jar. Soak them in warm water for 20–25 minutes (or in cold water for several hours), squeeze dry and discard the hard stalks before use. Fresh mushrooms, which are quite different in fragrance and texture, do not make a good substitute.

Cooking oil In China the most commonly used cooking oil is made from soya beans, peanuts, rape seeds, sunflower seeds or cotton seeds. Pork or chicken fat is sometimes used, but never butter or dripping.

Five-spice powder A highly piquant mixture of star anise, fennel seeds, cloves, cinnamon and Sichuan pepper, which should be used very sparingly. It will keep indefinitely in an airtight container.

Ginger root Fresh ginger root, sold by weight, should be peeled and sliced, finely chopped or shredded before use. It will keep for weeks in a dry, cool place. Another way of keeping it fresh is to peel it, place it in a jar and cover with pale dry sherry; seal and store in the fridge.

Golden needles Dried tiger lily (*Hemerocallis fulva*) buds. They should be soaked in warm water for 10–20 minutes and the hard stems removed. Often served with wood ears.

Hoi Sin sauce Also known as barbecue sauce, this is made from soya beans, sugar, flour, vinegar, salt, garlic, chilli and sesame seed oil. Sold in cans or jars, it will keep in the refrigerator for several months.

Monosodium glutamate Also known as 'taste essence' (*veh t'sin* in Chinese), MSG is a chemical compound widely used in restaurants to enhance the natural flavours of ingredients that have passed their prime. Unnecessary when cooking fresh food.

Oyster sauce A thickish soya-based sauce used as a flavouring in Cantonese cooking. Sold in bottles, it will keep in the refrigerator for months.

Prawns In Britain, small prawns are usually sold ready-cooked, either in their shells or peeled. These are not ideal for Chinese cooking, so try to get the larger, uncooked variety sometimes known as king prawns. They are usually available frozen in their shells, either whole or headless. They should always be thoroughly defrosted.

Rice wine Chinese rice wine, made from glutinous rice, is also known as 'yellow wine' (*huang jiu* or *chiew* in Chinese), because of its golden amber colour. The best variety is called Shao Hsing or Shaoxing, and comes from south-east China. A

good dry or medium sherry is an acceptable substitute.

Sesame paste Also known as Sesame sauce, this highly aromatic, rich and tasty sauce resembles clay in colour and consistency. Sold in jars, it must be stirred well to make it into a creamy paste before use. Peanut butter creamed with sesame seed oil is a possible substitute.

Sesame seed oil Sold in bottles, this is widely used in China as a 'garnish' rather than for cooking. The refined yellow sesame oil sold in Middle-Eastern stores has less flavour and is not so aromatic, so it is not a very satisfactory substitute.

Shrimps, dried Available in different sizes, dried shrimps have been salted and dried in the sun. They should be soaked in warm water for 25–30 minutes, then drained and rinsed before use. Dried, they will keep almost indefinitely in an airtight container.

Soy sauce Sold in bottles or cans, this popular Chinese sauce is used both for cooking and at table. Light soy sauce has more flavour than the sweeter, darker kind, which gives food a rich colour.

Water chestnuts These are actually the roots of a vegetable (*Heleocharis tuberosa*), not nuts at all. They are available fresh or in cans, but the canned variety retain only part of their texture and flavour. In a screw-top jar, they will keep for about a month in the refrigerator.

Wood ears Also known as 'cloud ears', these are dried black fungus (*Auricularia auricula*). Sold in plastic bags in Oriental stores, they should be soaked in warm water for 25–30 minutes, then rinsed in fresh water before use. They have a crunchy texture and a mild but subtle flavour.

Yellow bean paste A thick paste made from salted, fermented yellow soya beans crushed with flour and sugar. It is sold in cans or jars; once the can is opened, the contents should be transferred to a screw-top jar. It will then keep in the refrigerator for months.

INDEX

C

Cabbage
    stir-fried green cabbage 48
Cantonese stuffed bean curd in oyster
    sauce 73
Cashew nuts
    Sichuan 'kung-po' chicken with cashew
      nuts 80
Casseroles
    Chinese leaves and bean curd
      casserole 53
    seafood casserole 60
    vegetarian casserole 45
Cauliflower
    steamed cauliflower in cream sauce 53
Celery
    kidney and celery salad 25
    shredded chicken with celery 76
    'three whites' in cream sauce 52
Chicken
    braised chicken in brown sauce 77
    chicken and beansprout soup 17
    chicken and ham salad with mustard
      sauce 30
    chicken and mushrooms 79
    chicken cubes with cucumber 84
    chicken fu-yung 76
    chicken slices and vegetables 80
    Chinese 'paella' 63
    diced chicken with green peppers 84
    drunken chicken 81
    Hunan chicken in spicy sauce 81
    red-cooked chicken 77
    roast chicken Canton-style 82
    shredded chicken with celery 76
    Sichuan bon-bon chicken 29
    Sichuan 'kung-po' chicken with cashew
      nuts 80
    soy-braised chicken 29
    steamed chicken with Chinese
      mushrooms 82
    three-flavour soup 20
Chinese cuisine 7–9

Chinese leaves
    braised Chinese leaves with
      mushrooms 49
    Chinese leaves and bean curd
      casserole 53
    Chinese leaves and mushroom
      soup 14
    'lions' heads' 93
    mixed vegetable salad with spicy
      dressing 25
    'three whites' in cream sauce 52
Chinese 'paella' 63
Chow mein 110
Courgettes
    courgettes with red peppers 55
Crab
    crab with spring onions and ginger 70
    egg fu-yung with prawns or
      crabmeat 60
    'lions' heads' 93
    sweetcorn and crabmeat soup 21
Crystal-boiled pork with crushed garlic
    sauce 32
Cucumber
    chicken cubes with cucumber 84
    sliced lamb and cucumber soup 20

D

Duck
    boiled duck Peking-style 87
    eight-treasure duck 87
    roast duck Peking-style 85
    Shanghai soya duck 24

SUPPLIERS

Ken Lo's Kitchen
14 Eccleston Street
London SW1

◆

Cheong Leen Supermarket
4–10 Tower Street
Cambridgeshire Close
London WC2

◆

Loon Fung Provisions
42/43 Gerrard Street
London W1

◆

Chung Nam Provisions
162 Bromsgrove Street
Birmingham 5

◆

Chung Wah Trading Centre
31/32 Great Georges Square
Liverpool 1

◆

Chung Ying Supermarket
63 Cambridge Street
Glasgow

◆

Yau's Chinese Foodstore
9 St. Mary's Street
Southampton